Instant Surround Sound

Jeffrey P. Fisher

CMPBooks
San Francisco, CA

Published by CMP Books
an imprint of CMP Media LLC
600 Harrison Street, 6th Floor, San Francisco, CA 94107 USA
Tel: 415-947-6615; Fax: 415-947-6015
www.cmpbooks.com
email: books@cmp.com

Distributed in the U.S. by:
Publishers Group West
1700 Fourth Street
Berkeley, CA 94710
1-800-788-3123

Distributed in Canada by:
Jaguar Book Group
100 Armstrong Avenue
Georgetown, Ontario M6K 3E7 Canada
905-877-4483

For individual orders and for information on special discounts for quantity orders, please contact:
CMP Books Distribution Center, 6600 Silacci Way, Gilroy, CA 95020
email: cmp@rushorder.com; Web: www.cmpbooks.com

ISBN: 1-57820-246-9

Dedication

It might seem unusual for an author to dedicate a book to three people he's never met. Nevertheless, these three legends have had (and continue to have) a profound impact on my music and sound career: Sir George Martin, Ben Burtt, and Gary Rydstrom. Thank you all for opening up my ears to the possibilities.

—Jeffrey P. Fisher

Acknowledgments

Once again I'd like to thank Douglas and Mannie at VASST for their continued support of my work. Kudos also to the whole CMP team who make these books a reality. Also, very special thanks to Tony Santona for his illustrations used throughout the book.

—Jeffrey P. Fisher

Contents

Foreword

Welcome to the huge world of surround sound. Surround sound has been available to professionals for many years, but is just now coming of age in the desktop authoring world as a common choice for multimedia and music authors.

Surround sound isn't a simple matter of just taking a stereo or mono audio track and porting it to 6 different locations, it's about understanding balance, relative power, phasing, realistic placement techniques, downmixing, resampling, encoding, compression, equalization, and so much, much more. This book from Jeffrey P. Fisher is about the discovery process that makes all these seemingly complex subjects become clear and concise.

What few books are currently available on surround sound are essentially white papers with pretty colored covers. The Instant Series books aren't designed to talk down to readers; they're designed as a book you can settle comfortably back in your computer chair or other favorite reading place, read this book, and not find yourself puzzling over numbers, tables, or other challenges. The purpose of this book is to immerse you in the world of surround sound and get you moving down the path of making a great sounding blockbuster hit!

Jeffrey P. Fisher has a knack for making the comprehensive appear second nature, and doing so in a manner that is smooth, sensible, and most importantly, workflow-oriented.

This is Jeffrey's third project in the VASST Instant Series, and we're confident you'll find this a great read, just like his previous efforts.

From us here at VASST, we thank you for your support of our training materials, and invite you to view our other training products both for purchase and for free, at www.vasst.com.

Douglas Spotted Eagle
Managing Producer

Mannie Frances
Managing Director

Introduction

Perception Conception

The primary reason to use multichannel sound is to enhance the listening experience. Surround sound helps both music and visual producers deepen the realism and involve the audience further. For example, the approach of a rescue helicopter sent to save the movie hero has greater impact when it first appears in the distance behind the audience, flies its way to the front of the viewing room, and then across the screen. Similarly, music recordings have more intimacy when the singer's voice moves about the room in the same manner she might on a live stage. Surround sound also enhances live performances presented on CD/DVD by placing the listener in the auditorium, keeping the performance on stage and the original audience and room sounds in the surrounds.

Surround sound works because of the four ways we humans perceive sound:

- Audible periphery—each ear functioning as an independent receiver
- Binaural perception—hearing the same sound with both ears
- Spatial perception—perceiving both where we are and where other sound elements are in space

- Cognitive perception—how well we perceive and localize sounds

The ear works by collecting sound, via the outside of the ear called the pinna, and sending it down the ear canal. The ear drum, a piece of tightly stretched skin, sits at the end of the canal and vibrates when struck with sound energy. The three bones of the ossicles—the hammer, anvil, and stirrup—transfer this vibration into the cochlea or inner ear. Sound energy from the ossicles creates an analogous wave pattern in the cochlea. Tiny hairs in the cochlea are sensitive to the movement and send an electrochemical response to the brain, which perceives the sound.

Our head helps us to localize sound sources because sounds arrive at our ears at different times. Because of the distance between the ears, sounds can arrive approximately .7 milliseconds apart. Our brain assumes that first-arriving sounds are the loudest sounds, although this may not be the case.

We perceive only loudness and pitch for all the sounds that we hear. However, this perception isn't that precise. Instead we tend to recognize sounds as objects or sources and not focus on specifics of loudness and pitch. Because of this, a surround sound mix often allows for more intimate, quieter overall sound as there are more point sources to deliver unique sounds for the ear to perceive. This can be used to the advantage of both music mixes and audio for video mixes.

When preparing to mix, keep these perceptual contributors in mind. Compared with two-speaker, conventional stereo, surround sound offers:

- Better perception of object and sound location. Listeners more readily identify the general direction from which sounds are initiated.

- A different loudness balance over stereo playback alone. The volume can be lower yet provide more enjoyment due to perception of placement.

- More accurate perception of tone due to the additional placement options of sound sources.

- Significantly greater perception of ambience. The audience can be more immersed in the listening field.

- More involved listener perception of sound points. Keep in mind that more speakers equals greater perceptive involvement.

- A greater awareness of the quality of the mix, both individual components and as a whole.

Quality Control

Although this book deals directly with the quality of the mix and how to record, process, and deliver the audio to the listener, it's important to address the quality of your recordings, too. When delivering your mix in surround, low-quality components such as inexpensive microphones, preamps, and other equipment used in audio processing become more apparent. The listener is more aware of individual sounds spread out over the listening space. For example, a mix containing low-frequency noise due to rumble might be easily masked by other sound elements in a two-speaker stereo mix. In a 5.1 mix, however, there are now four additional locations for that noise to be heard; it may be exposed and more prevalent in the multichannel environment.

Additionally, consider using more elemental ambiences to cover up or mask weak recordings. For example, a poorer quality sound can mask problems in the mix such as adding wind noise to create a constant "room tone" in an outdoor scene. The wind helps mask other noises in the mix.

Don't be afraid to supplant existing ambience or environmental sounds with your own. For instance, a forest scene with great dialog may also have a few crickets or other sounds on the production track. Rather than attempting to clean it up, augment the ambience instead. Lay these tones into your mix and craft a better experience. If you anchor the dialog to the center channel, and place the ambient element around the surround field, the audience accepts that they are in a forest setting with sound all around them. Most importantly, their attention focuses on the dialog, which should help mask any other sounds that may creep into that track, such as the cricket noises.

Surround can also work in our favor when the mix has problems. For example, if a car drives by during a critical point in a scene and it cannot be totally mixed out of the dialog track, find or create a recording of a similar car-by. Place this drive-by in the rear speakers. At the critical segment, modify the dialog EQ to cut the car element from the main dialog track while enhancing those same frequencies in the rear channel's car-by. Mixed properly with good balance, the audience will not be aware that you've got two different car drive-bys taking place. They'll know only that one is in the rear speakers and that shades of it are heard in the center or dialog location. Dynamic panning of the elements can help enhance the effect, too.

Chapter 1

Surround History 101

First there was monaural recording (mono for short) with its single speaker playing the sounds of our world. By 1877, Edison's crude cylinder-based phonograph was a huge leap forward for both recording and reproducing sound. A decade later, the Gramophone introduced shellac disks that could be mass-duplicated and distributed. It wasn't until 1948 that 45s and LPs emerged on vinyl.

Bell Labs experimented with stereo recording and playback in the 1930s. These early attempts routed two microphones to two separate speakers. Initial stereo radio broadcasts occurred sporadically during the 1950s. However, it took until the 1960s for stereo recordings to be released on vinyl LPs. Stereo TV arrived in the late 1970s. That same decade, the music industry flirted with quadraphonic sound—four speakers placed in the corners of a room. Unfortunately, its high cost and lack of a standardized format precluded it from catching on.

Many attempts to synchronize moving pictures and sound failed until the Vitaphone played Al Jolson's music performances for the ears of amazed moviegoers. The Vitaphone was essentially a Gramophone hooked up to the film projector. Soon after, the marriage of the soundtrack to the film itself become possible. Sound picked up by a microphone modulated a light source that exposed film. This optical sound became the film standard and is still present on all films released today. Mono dominated for years until *Fantasia* brought a unique experience to the movies playing stereo using three front speakers and a mono effects track using two rear speakers to envelop the audience.

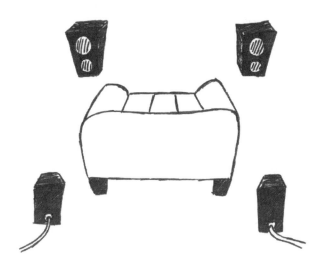

Magnetic tape as a recording medium started being used in 1940 and continued to dominate film, TV, and music sound recording until digital recording became viable. Tape is still the choice for many, especially for music recording, but digital is obviously heavily entrenched.

The compact disc (CD), introduced in 1981, spelled the demise of both vinyl and cassette as a consumer format. Today, MP3 and other Internet-friendly formats compete for dominance in the music-delivery arena.

TV's unfounded threat to drive patrons away from movie theaters forced the film industry into multichannel sound during the 1950s. Larger screens built to accommodate widescreen Cinerama and Cinemascope movies needed equally larger soundtracks. Hollywood's solution was to add a third dedicated center channel to the two stereo speakers and a special effects channel at the rear of the theater to help "surround" the audience.

The development of 70mm film created space on the film for six discrete analog soundtracks: left, left-center, center, right-center, right and a single rear channel for effects. Dolby Laboratories embraced what would evolve into the 5.1 format. Additionally, Dolby improved standard 35mm film sound with Dolby Stereo, Dolby Surround, and then Dolby Pro Logic. These last two formats used specially matrixed and encoded tracks to represent the Left-Center-Right and a single mono surround channel (LCRS). Many movies released on VHS had these soundtracks, which first brought theater sound to the home.

Batman Returns **carried the first Dolby Digital soundtrack.**

The first movie to use a DTS soundtrack was *Jurassic Park.*

Later, Dolby's digitally encoded recordings squeezed 5.1 onto standard 35mm film in the space between the sprocket holes. By 1992, Dolby Digital 5.1 was born for the movies, using their AC-3 compression which soon after became standardized as the DVD specification. All DVD players must be able to decode Dolby Digital 5.1. They must also be able to deliver Dolby Surround, stereo, and mono from that single 5.1 soundtrack. Dolby Digital 5.1 is also part of the HDTV specification.

Competition at the movies came from Digital Theater Sound (DTS) in 1993 with separate CDs that play in sync with the picture (shades of Vitaphone's past). DTS playback by DVD players is optional. Another format, Sony Dynamic Digital Sound (SDDS) is a 7.1 system with five speakers in the front. DTS-ES and Dolby Surround EX both add a center surround channel to the mix.

On the music side, two competing formats, DVD-Audio and Super Audio Compact Disc (SACD) both deliver high-quality 5.1. Unfortunately, not all DVD players are capable of reproducing the formats, a situation that hints at the incompatibility problems of yesterday's Quad format. Some DVD player manufacturers are starting to support both formats, though. However, getting surround sound into automobiles may be the key to these formats' longevity.

Today, the Dolby Digital 5.1 format has emerged as the standard for the home theater and home listening environment, the success of the DVD format with its vastly improved picture and sound quality being the primary motivating factor. The sale of home theater speaker systems and larger television screens continues to rise, too. While movie theaters may continue to improve on the aural experience, the majority of homeowners will most likely be reluctant to add additional components to already crowded family rooms and home theaters. With that in mind, 5.1 is likely to pervade the music and sound industry for many years to come.

Numeric Roots

Monaural (1.0) uses a single speaker to deliver sound. There isn't a sense of spaciousness, because all sound comes from a single point in space.

Stereo (2.0 or L/R) uses two speakers spaced apart, which creates a virtual sound field between them. The stereo experience has a sense of depth and space to it, with many sounds seemingly emanating from the center even though no speaker is actually there. This phenomenon is called the phantom center.

Unfortunately, the stereo effect works only when you are positioned in the sweet spot between the speakers. Outside this area, the stereo effect is greatly diminished pushing toward a monaural sound. Though the spaciousness of the stereo effect is often more pleasing than mono, the effect originates from a single direction, usually in front of you. There is no sense of being *in* the recording.

Adding a center channel (3.0 or C) to the stereo pair was a Hollywood invention to solve the problem of being outside the stereo sweet spot. Using its own discrete speaker anchored the film dialog to the center of the movie screen no matter where the audience sat in the theater. Reinforcing the phantom center gives better directional cues for people sitting outside the stereo sweet spot, too.

Two additional channels (5.0) positioned to the rear immerses the audience into the sound field. These discrete left and right surrounds (LsRs) expand the depth and spaciousness of the stereo effect into a full 360-degree circle that envelopes the audience. As a consequence, the surround effect greatly expands the sweet spot so that more of the audience can hear the result.

"Boom channel" or "baby boom" is slang for the LFE.

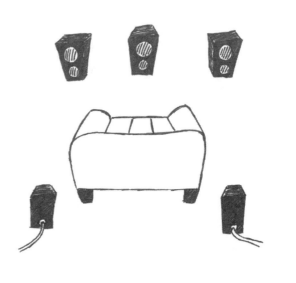

The final part of the surround equation is the dedicated Low Frequency Enhancement (LFE) channel (.1) positioned in the front near the center channel. The point-one designation is because it has 1/10th the bandwidth of the other full-range speakers. The purpose of the LFE is to provide *additional* bass content. Good LFE effects are more felt than heard, such as explosions from the latest Hollywood blockbuster.

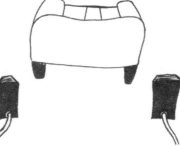

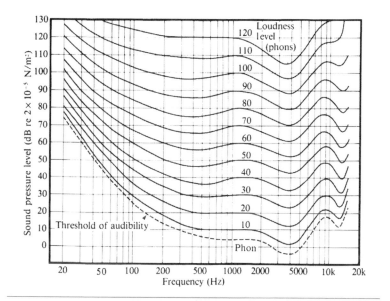

The Fletcher-Munson equal loudness contours plot the ear's frequency response at given listening levels. They reveal that the ear is less sensitive to low frequencies. The LFE provides additional bass to the experience to compensate and is set up to play back 10dB louder than the other five speakers.

Matrix or Discrete

There are two flavors of surround sound. The matrix approach uses special encoding tricks that add the multichannel information to the stereo mix. Decoders in the listening environment recreate the experience.

However, the format is not without its share of problems. Some material may be routed to the wrong speakers. The unpredictable results even vary by program material. Common matrix formats include Dolby Surround Pro Logic and SRS Labs Circle Surround. Dolby Pro Logic is a four-channel system with a monaural surround, essentially LCRS.

The second flavor is discrete surround, which keeps the individual channels separate throughout the encoding and decoding phase. The individual outputs are then routed to their respective speakers, recreating the original mix exactly. Both DTS Coherent Acoustics Audio and Dolby Digital (AC-3) are discrete surround formats, as are DVD-Audio and SACD.

Because of its predictable playback, discrete surround is the most common and recommended format for delivering surround. In fact, the Producers and Engineers wing of the Recording Academy (www.grammy.com) recommend only discrete surround sound in their white paper, "Recommendations for Surround Sound Production."

Presented in
SRS(●)®
Circle Surround 5.1

PRODUCERS &
ENGINEERS WING

The Recording Academy's Producers & Engineers Wing

Recommendations For
Surround Sound Production

Custom Template	?|X

Template: 5.1 Surround DVD

Description: Audio: 448 Kbps, 48,000 Hz, 5.1 Surround
Main Audio Service: Complete main
Use this setting for 5.1 Surround DVD soundtracks.

Input filtering
☐ Digital de-emphasis
☑ DC high-pass filter
☑ Bandwidth low-pass filter
☑ LFE low-pass filter

Surround channel processing
☑ 90-degree phase shift
☐ 3 dB attenuation

Dynamic range compression
Line mode profile: Film: Standard
RF mode profile: Film: Standard
☐ RF overmodulation protection

DOLBY DIGITAL

Audio Service / Bitstream / Ext. Bitstream \ Preprocessing

OK   Cancel

The AC-3 Thang

It is primarily the Dolby AC-3 codec that brings 5.1 surround sound to the masses. Developed in 1992 to carry multichannel soundtracks on 35mm film, it has since been adapted to DTV, HDTV, and DVD. The format supports both stereo and discrete 5.1 multi-channel audio streams. AC-3 stands for audio compression, generation three. The format uses encoding techniques to compress audio files significantly, with minimal impact on the resulting sound's quality.

Dolby Digital AC-3 is a high-resolution spectral envelope coding technique and hybrid forward/backward adaptive bit allocation technique. Essentially that means it uses flexible perceptual encoding to compress audio data. Perceptual encoding relies on the concept of psychoacoustic masking, meaning that some sounds cover up or mask others. The encoder then only has to allocate bits to the foreground sound.

The process works by filtering the audio stream into discreet bands. The encoder then looks at the dominant frequencies at any given point in time per frequency band. The encoder allocates bits only to what's most prominent. Sometimes no bits are allocated for a specific band. Ultimately, this selective encoding process reduces file size considerably.

AC-3 also supports specific metadata that accompanies the data stream. These metadata tell the AC-3 decoder how to handle the surround sound. Configuring the metadata becomes important during the encoding step, which is discussed in Chapter Eight.

The Dolby encoder technology was first a hardware device but has since been mostly replaced by software equivalents. Dolby now licenses its AC-3 encoder to a variety of software vendors for people to use to encode their own surround sound projects. These software products typically include the necessary tools for authoring in surround sound, too.

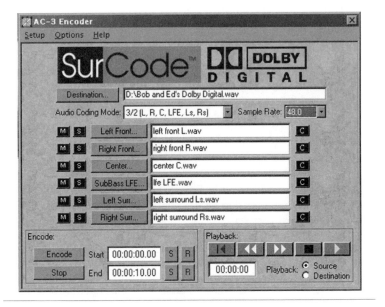

DTS Coherent Acoustics Audio

Another encoder available for both PC and Mac is the DTS Pro Series Surround Encoder. This standalone package handles the encoding process of imported files. You still need an audio or video application that exports the necessary files.

Delivering Surround

There are several delivery formats for surround sound:

- DVD—the DVD specification demands support for Dolby 5.1 on all players.

- DVD-A—this special audio-only version of the DVD specification supports high-quality multichannel sound.

- SACD—This is another audio-only disc format that offers high-quality multichannel sound.

- DTV—Digital Television supports 18 different video formats ranging from standard definition (SD) up to various high-definition (HD) iterations. The DTV audio format specification is just one: Dolby AC-3 in both stereo and 5.1.

- Windows Media 9 (and above)—supports delivering high-quality 5.1 material. WMV9 also supports delivering high-definition (HD) video along with the surround soundtrack.

Chapter 2

Recording Surround

Surround sound projects are typically built through a careful blending of mono and stereo recordings. Through volume and placement, you immerse your listening audience into a unique aural environment and experience. Increasingly, projects are being recorded directly to the discrete format at the source. Capturing a live musical performance, for example, directly to the 5.1 format results in a recording that captures the original sound of the room. Supplementing the 5.1 recording with dedicated spot mics provides additional control over the final blend.

Recording Chain

Recording acoustic sounds requires a simple chain of components: microphone, microphone preamp, and recorder. Multichannel recordings require an equivalent number of mics, preamps, and discrete recording tracks.

The higher the quality of the component parts, the better the resulting sound recordings will be.

A Little About Mics

Inside every microphone is a small, thin sheet of metal, called the diaphragm, which vibrates analogously to the sound waves that strike it. The microphone converts this vibrating pattern into an electrical signal that can be recorded. There are three main types of microphones: dynamic, condenser, and ribbon.

Dynamic mics are tiny electrical generators. They work by connecting the vibrating diaphragm to a coil of wire. This wire surrounds a fixed magnet. As the diaphragm vibrates, it moves the coil through the magnetic field generating low-power alternating current (AC).

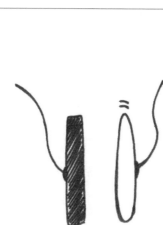

Ribbon microphones suspend a thin, corrugated piece of metal between a U-shaped magnet. As sound strikes the ribbon, it vibrates, producing alternating current just as the dynamic microphone does. Ribbon mics are fragile and particularly vulnerable to wind damage.

Condenser mics have two metal diaphragms spaced closely together with an insulating air space between them. One plate is fixed; the other is able to move freely. Positive voltage from an electrical supply is sent to one plate and negative voltage to the other. As sound strikes the diaphragm (the moveable plate) it vibrates, moving closer and farther away from the fixed plate. This changes the voltage, creating a variable alternating current analogous to the sound waves striking it.

Condenser microphones need a power source to function properly. This power may come from a battery, a separate power supply, or as phantom power provided by an audio mixers. Condenser microphones are far more sensitive to subtle sound changes and excel at capturing the finer nuances of sound.

Pick-Up Patterns

Our ears are rather adept at tuning out unwanted noise. Mics, however, can't discriminate sounds like our ears; they hear everything! However, some mics are more sensitive in certain directions than others, and this pattern of sensitivity is called its pick-up or polar pattern.

Omni-directional microphones pick up sound equally well in all directions.

Uni-directional or cardioid micro-phones are more sensitive in one di-rection, having a heart-shaped pattern extending out from the mic's front.

Hyper-cardioid mics narrow and elongate this pick-up pattern, further rejecting even more off-axis sound.

Cardioids reject off-axis sound, which can help reduce environmental noise in certain settings.

Super-cardioids have a tight pattern and are more commonly called shot-gun microphones

Bi-directional microphones have a figure-eight pattern.

Pressure-zone microphones (PZM) have a hemispherical pick-up pattern.

Mics come in a variety of designs. Handheld mics are suitable for singers and speakers, studio mics should be mounted on a stand, while lavalieres clip on to clothing. Shotguns are usually suspended from a fish pole boom.

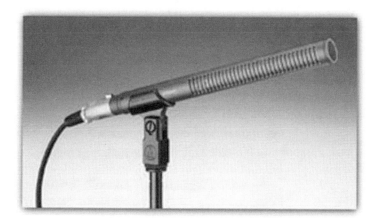

Boosting and Recording the Signal

Microphones put out a tiny amount of electricity, so the signal must be boosted before it can be used by other audio components. This microphone preamplifier or preamp for short can be a standalone product or part of a more complete audio mixer. Clearly, surround recording requires five or six preamps (one for each mic).

Recording in surround requires a recorder capable of handling the six discrete tracks. This recorder could be a dedicated hardware unit or a software-based system that supports multiple, simultaneous channels.

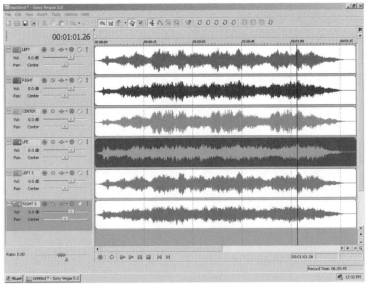

Mono and Stereo Microphone Techniques

Creating a mono recording of a sound event is the easiest of all recordings to make. Choose a high-quality mic, preamp, and recorder. Aim the mic at the source, set the level, press record, and go. Unfortunately, the playback, while faithful to the sound source, will lack the sense of depth and spaciousness that our ears originally heard.

Because we humans have two ears, the next challenge is to capture the stereophonic quality that we experience daily. That means two separate mics and two separate recording tracks. There are three common stereo micing techniques. Other stereo microphone techniques are typically variations of these three primary methods.

The spaced omni method uses two matched omni-directional mics spaced apart at least three times the distance to the source being recorded.

XY positions a matched pair of cardioids close together but pointed in opposite directions, 90 degrees away from center.

ORTF, positions two matched cardioids, pointed in a V pattern 17cm and 110 degrees apart.

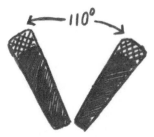

There are also dedicated stereo microphones, such as the Audio Technica AT-853 and the Rode NT-4.

Binaural recording is an interesting stereo technique that uses microphones positioned in the "ears" of a dummy head. The resulting recordings are surprisingly open and realistic, especially when listening to playback on headphones.

The Decca Tree is yet another stereo microphone technique that uses three omni-directional microphones: left, right, and center. All three mics face forward and form an equilateral triangle with the center mic at the apex. Alternately, cardioids can be substituted.

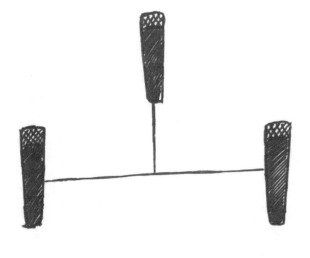

Localization vs. Space

Stereo recording is a trade-off between having a deep and wide stereo image and the precise location of a sound source between the two speakers. Some techniques accentuate the sense of space but make it hard to discern the specific position of elements within that space. The sound is open and full but lacks definition. Other microphone techniques provide a precise picture of the sound sources, but sacrifice the stereo effect somewhat. For example, XY micing is strong on localization but loses the spatial impression. ORTF is weak on localization but strong in how it presents a sense of stereo space.

Select only one:

- Deep, wide, luscious stereo, or

- Good localization of sound sources

With surround comes the added spatial impression called envelopment—literally immersing the audience with sound. Again, striking a balance between localization (a sound's specific position) and the depth and space of envelopment is the key when recording surround and ultimately when mixing it, too.

Surround Micing Techniques

Currently, surround micing is an off-shoot of the stereo microphone techniques just discussed. For example, you can use two ORTF setups, one pointed toward the sound source, the other pointed away. Then route the recording of the front-facing pair to the left and right speakers and the rear-facing pair to the left and right surround speakers (LsRs) to recreate the space. A dedicated center mic could also be added to this approach.

Alternately, starting with a Decca tree, using all cardioids, and then adding two rear-facing microphones provides five discrete channels.

A variation would be to angle the front left and right mics and the rear surround mics to closely approximate the recommended surround playback configuration (discussed later in this book). The front and rears could also be separated in space.

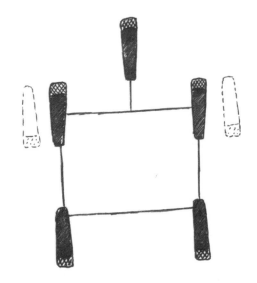

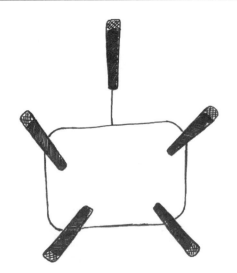

There are also dedicated surround microphones, such as the Holophone H2Pro (www.holophone.com), that allow for easier positioning and use while maintaining the unique ambience of multichannel recording. This mic is practically a surround variation on the binaural principal.

Holophone offers a 5.1 demo DVD that features several different H2 recordings.

These approaches all neglect the LFE channel, though a sixth microphone, specifically an omni, could be employed to capture this channel.

Some Hollywood soundtracks use these 5.1 techniques to capture orchestral scores. Increasingly, live recordings of musical acts are using 5.1 to capture the audience perspective. However, most engineers supplement these "ambience" recordings with spot mics dedicated to individual performances. For example, there may be dedicated mics on each main instrument and singer routed to separate recording tracks. These join the 5.1 recording, providing more mixing control during post-production.

Chapter 3

Up and Running

Whether your surround sound projects originate as discrete 5.1 recordings or come together using a variety of mono and stereo recordings, the post-production requirements are essentially identical. A combination of computer hardware and software coupled to audio speakers is what's needed to implement surround in a desktop environment.

Computer Hardware and Software

The choice of Mac or PC depends entirely on the software you select to mix and master your surround sound projects. If you are just starting out, my recommendation is to find the software you want to use and then buy the platform it runs on. If you are already established, you either have to find surround authoring software or it is already included with other software you currently use.

Look for software that thinks the way you do. Don't be swayed by what other people say you should use. Download the demos, give them a test drive, and then make your decision. This method may take a little more time, but you'll save future headaches from fighting with software that doesn't mirror and complement your working style.

Here's a short list of software tools that currently support surround sound

- Adobe Audition
- Avid*
- BIAS Deck
- Mark of the Unicorn Digital Performer
- Apple Final Cut Pro*
- Apple (formerly E-magic) Logic Audio
- Adobe Premiere Pro*
- Digidesign Pro Tools
- Cakewalk SONAR
- Sony ACID Pro
- Sony Vegas*
- Steinberg Nuendo

*denotes non-linear video editing software (NLE)

All of these programs require a robust computer system. Refer to your software's system requirements for specific minimum hardware configurations. However, these minimums usually result in poor performance. I highly suggest choosing faster processors and additional RAM far above these minimum specifications.

Keep your OS and programs on a dedicated hard drive and then add additional dedicated drives for storing your audio, video, and other media. These hard drives can be internal or external, USB or FireWire.

If your video work is destined to play on a TV, checking it on an external video monitor is critical. With surround audio monitors properly set up, watching on a external monitor while mixing surround is an ideal working arrangement.

Control Devices

Many people prefer working with hardware instead of the point-and-click of the mouse. Some surround authoring software supports using external hardware, too. The popular Mackie Universal Control adds motorized faders, knobs, buttons, and switches that can be configured to operate a myriad of software-based controls.

A hardware joystick can make surround positioning easier. Some are built into external hardware devices, or you may be able to use a standard gaming joystick.

Soundcard Options

Working with surround requires a soundcard with six discrete output channels. Make sure those six outputs are available simultaneously and in a format you can use. You want line-level output on XLR, 1/4" or 1/8" jacks. The connector choice depends on your monitor speaker configuration, discussed below. You can choose internal, PCI soundcards or external components, either USB or FireWire.

Specifications also vary by manufacturer. Some soundcards support only 16-bit sound (the CD standard), while others provide higher quality 24-bit. If you work with 24-bit files or need to make higher-quality recordings, consider a 24-bit soundcard.

Audio Monitors

Mixing and monitoring surround sound requires six dedicated speakers, one of them a subwoofer capable of reproducing extreme low frequencies. There are two choices.

Passive speakers get their power from a separate amplifier. As such, you would need multiple amplifiers or an amplifier specifically designed to work with discrete surround. This amplifier must have the necessary six inputs and six speaker connections.

Alternately, powered speakers, often called active monitors, have built-in amplifiers. They connect directly to the soundcard outputs.

There are also hybrid systems, such as the M-Audio LX-4, which houses its six amplifiers in the subwoofer sending discrete signals to the remaining five passive speakers.

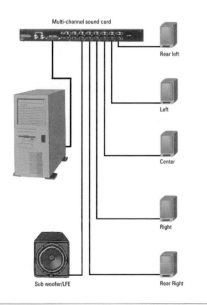

Select high-quality speakers designed for critical music monitoring. They should all be exactly the same brand and model. Make sure the speakers are direct radiator types (these are the most common) and not a dipole design. Make sure the speakers are magnetically shielded to avoid interference with nearby computers or television monitors.

Get five identical self-powered, mid-field monitors along with a matching self-powered subwoofer.

Both the Dolby and Recording Academy recommendations state that the five main speakers—stereo L/R, surround L/R, and dedicated center—should be full-range, matched speakers. This means each speaker should be capable of reproducing the entire frequency range from 20 to 20,000 Hertz (Hz). The sixth LFE speaker only needs to effectively reproduce frequencies below 120Hz. For proper surround mixing, the LFE is discrete and dedicated only to additional bass effects. The other five speakers reproduce full-range sounds, including the bass.

Avoid the inexpensive 5.1 computer speakers. These are designed for gamers, not serious surround projects. However, they may be useful as a second set of speakers to check compatibility. I also recommend having a consumer surround sound system, preferably a bass managed one, installed in a typical home listening environment for further testing and checking of your mixes.

Most consumer systems use smaller, limited bandwidth satellite speakers and route all the bass content to a subwoofer. This approach is called bass management. And while it is sufficient for home theater playback, it is not the preferred method for effective surround sound authoring. This is also a point of so much confusion. In consumer systems, the subwoofer does double duty, providing both the deep bass content missing from the satellites *and* the LFE sounds. Bass management will be explored in greater detail later.

Basic Audio Studio Setup

Though specific placement is detailed below, keep these general restrictions in mind. Be sure the speakers are wired correctly and in phase. Keep the connecting cables as short as possible and match the lengths to all speakers. Choose high-quality wire. Generally, heavier, thicker cable equals better cable.

Place each of the five main speakers on rock-solid matching stands. Make sure the tweeters are at ear level and that there are *no* obstructions between the speakers and the listening position. The subwoofer can sit on the floor. Isolate each speaker from the surface upon which it rests using rigid foam such as Auralex MoPads.

Place the speakers in the free field, sufficiently away from nearby walls. Three to five feet away from boundaries is an acceptable range. Speaker placement is symmetrical, which is somewhat contrary to conventional wisdom regarding control room design, which is mostly asymmetrical.

Also, unlike most stereo mixing environments, surround monitoring is best carried out in a room that is more "dead" or neutral sounding. Treat the room acoustics to reduce reverberation time and dampen the early reflections effectively. First reflections are particularly troublesome. As sound leaves the speakers it strikes the many surfaces of the room. These surfaces reflect sound back to the mixing position. Sometimes these sounds are in- or out-of-phase with the original sound, causing constructive and destructive interference. In short, the first reflections can affect what you hear in adverse ways.

Careful placement of broadband sound-absorbing material around and behind the speakers coupled to sufficient diffusion outside the surround sweet spot results in a more accurate mix. Products such as acoustic foam, bass traps, and diffusers provide solutions to common control room acoustical problems.

Here's a neat trick for dealing with those pesky first reflections. You need a good-sized hand mirror and an assistant. Sit at the mixing position. Have your assistant hold the mirror and move it along the room's main boundaries and surfaces (walls, ceiling, floor, large furniture). If you can see the front of a speaker in the mirror, that is a first reflection point for the sound coming from that speaker. This is an optimal location for broadband sound-absorbing material. Take your time and methodically check every surface for reflections and then treat the room accordingly based on what you discover.

Control room acoustics are beyond the scope of this book. Check out the free resources available from Auralex Acoustics (www.auralex. com or www. acoustics101. com).

Precise Speaker Placement

Speaker positioning is critical to having your surround mixes translate well to other listening systems and environments. Properly placing the speakers requires a reference point—the listening or mixing position. Room layout, equipment, and other factors dictate where you will sit for mixing and monitoring surround. Keep the previous tips in mind when selecting this position.

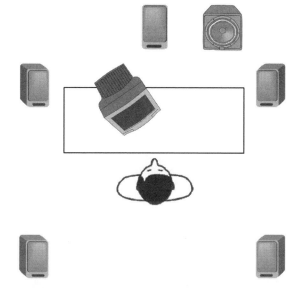

The recommendations for surround sound speaker placement come from the International Telecommunications Union (ITU) and their ITU Rec.775. The five main speakers form a circle with the mixing position at its center. This means the speakers will be the same distance from the listening position, optimally between six and eight feet.

The center speaker faces the listening position. The distance *between* the front left and right stereo speakers should equal the distance to the listening position. All three points—the L/R speakers and the mixing position—form an equilateral triangle. Angle the front left and right speakers in 30 degrees.

Place the surround speakers 110 degrees to 135 degrees from the center, also angled in. Steeper angles up to 150 degrees are acceptable for music mixing. Shallower angles are more suitable for film and TV surround mixing. Ideally the surrounds should be the same height as the front three, but it is acceptable for them to be slightly higher and aimed down toward the mixing position.

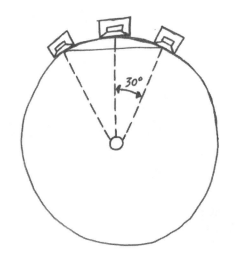

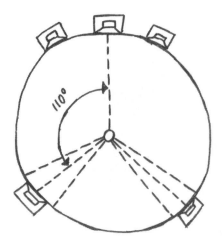

Place the subwoofer on the floor in the front slightly to one side of the center speaker. You may need to experiment to find the best placement for it. If applicable, set the subwoofer's low pass filter to 120Hz.

A simple way to position speakers is to use a mic stand, a length of string, and a protractor. Position the mic stand in the center of the listening position. Tie the string to the stand at ear height. Cut the string to the desired length for the speaker distance. Position the center speaker at the end of the string. Use the protractor for the angles and the string for the distance when placing the remaining four speakers.

Calibration Gear

After placement, properly calibrating the speakers also ensures that your surround mixes will sound as intended outside the mixing environment. Calibration requires an 80Hz sine wave test tone and pink noise. While sine waves are useful for calibrating electronic equipment, acoustic calibration uses pink noise, which sounds like an empty TV channel.

You also need either a Real-Time Analyzer (RTA) or a Sound Pressure Level (SPL) meter. Pink noise is available from tone generators, calibration CDs, and even many Hollywood DVD releases. RTAs are somewhat expensive, so for most people an SPL meter from Radio Shack suffices.

Alternately, create the test tone and pink noise needed using Sony Sound Forge. For the sine wave test tone, create a new, mono file (File>New). Click Tools>Synthesis>Simple and choose an 80Hz sine wave tone for 30 seconds or more.

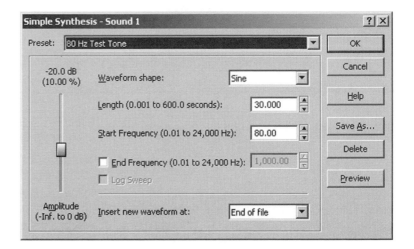

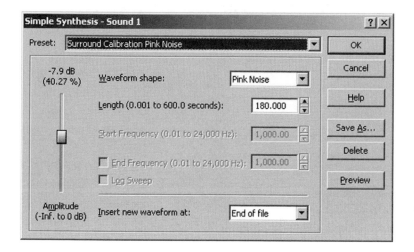

For pink noise, create an empty file, click Tools>Synthesis>Simple, and choose Pink Noise as the Waveform shape. Adjust the length to 180 seconds or so. Also, adjust the Amplitude to read –7.9dB. This creates at least three minutes of pink noise at –20dB (RMS) to use for calibrating your monitors.

It is important for the pink noise to be at 0 VU (Volume Unit), which equals –20dB RMS on digital full-scale meters. Zero VU is not the same as 0 on digital peak meters. Also, –20 on a digital peak meter does not equal 0 VU either. VU is more an average, or RMS (root, mean, squared) value, while digital meters typically read only peaks. Therefore, peak meters will read considerably higher than –20dBFS when playing back 0 VU pink noise.

There is also some merit to band-limiting the pink noise instead of using it at full bandwidth, because band-limited pink noise helps reduce the effects of room acoustics on the calibration procedures. In this case, use equalization controls to limit the pink noise to 500Hz to 2kHz for the five main speakers and in a different file, EQ the pink noise to 20Hz to 120Hz for the subwoofer.

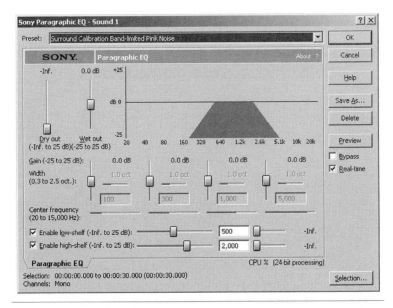

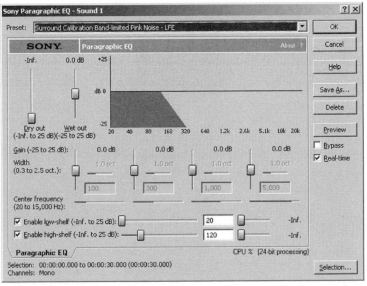

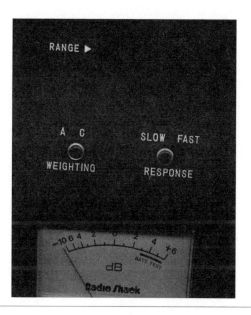

If you use an SPL meter, set it to C-weighting and slow response. Position it at ear level at the listening position with its microphone facing the center speaker. The RadioShack model even connects to a tripod for easy positioning.

Calibrating Speakers

Use the test tone to calibrate the subwoofer's acoustic phase alignment. Send the same 80Hz tone to both the left and right front speakers and the subwoofer at a moderately high level, such as 80dB. Note the level on the SPL meter. Use the sub's phase controls until you reach the loudest level. If the sub doesn't have phase controls, physically rotate it in 90-degree increments until the level reads the loudest on the SPL meter.

Periodically, check speaker placement and recalibrate to ensure that your surround mixing equipment runs at optimum levels.

Now set a reference sound pressure level for all six speakers. Generally, TV uses 79dB, film 83dB, and music 85dB as the reference SPL. Turn off all but one of the speakers. Route the 0 VU (–20dBFS RMS) band-limited pink noise to that speaker. Adjust its volume to read 83dB (or 79dB or 85dB) on the SPL meter (C-weighted, slow response) at the listening position. Repeat this procedure for the remaining four speakers.

For the LFE, use the 20Hz to 120Hz band-limited pink noise and adjust its volume to read 4dB higher than the other speakers: 87dB (or 83dB or 89dB). This technique delivers an LFE that is effectively 10dB louder than the other speakers to compensate for the ear's reduced sensitivity of low bass sounds. How can 4dB equal 10dB? The LFE is a limited-bandwidth channel, so the level works out when compared to the full speakers.

In some cases, the speakers employed may not have independent volume controls. Use the level controls available though the soundcard control panel when calibrating speakers. Note and save the settings.

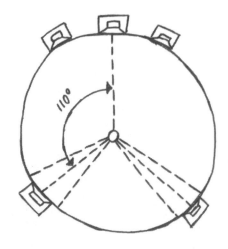

TV and Film Calibration Notes

As was mentioned above, television mixers prefer to work at the 79dB reference SPL (c-weighted, slow using −20dBFS RMS pink noise). This lower level makes balancing dialog easier. TV competes with far noisier home listening rooms. Dialog that sounds perfectly fine in a quiet studio referenced to 85dB may be too low in level and unintelligible when played back in most homes. Using the 79dB reference level forces the mixer to raise the dialog volume for better intelligibility more suited to home environments. If this is where most of your projects are destined, then consider recalibrating your monitors.

Also, U.S. theaters play back surround channels calibrated to 82dB (the fronts stay at 85dB). Some film mixers match this by calibrating the control room surrounds to 82dB, too. This means the surrounds will be 3dB louder than intended when played back on a system that references all five speakers to the same 85dB level. Both DTS Coherent Acoustics Audio and Dolby Digital AC-3 allow compensating for this fact during the encoding step, though.

Recommended calibration settings

- TV -- 79 dB

- Film -- 83 dB

- Music -- 85 dB

Chapter 4

Software Tools

With hardware in place, turn your attention to understanding the software tools available for surround sound mixing. While each software product has its own unique features, they all share common techniques and tools specific to surround sound work.

Multitracking

Critical to surround mixing is support for multiple audio tracks. Having access to a number of tracks gives greater control over the finished mix. Even if a field recording was made in 5.1, there is still a need for at least six tracks with the surround authoring program.

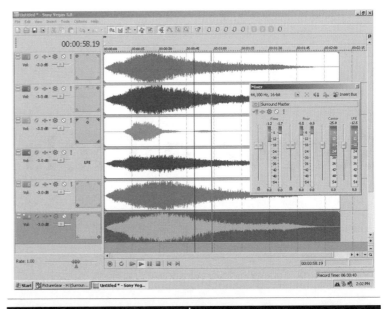

mono, stereo, or in some cases surround. These parts are spread over a number of tracks and must be balanced, or mixed, for the best presentation. You may take on the roles of sound designer, recording engineer, and surround mixer. It will be your responsibility to build the best soundtrack or music mix using the tools at your disposal.

For audio post projects, soundtrack elements comprise	For music projects, finished mixes comprise
• Dialog • Voice-over • Group walla • Sound effects • Foley • Backgrounds • Music	• Vocals • Drums and percussion • Rhythm instruments (guitars, bass, etc.) • Solo or lead instruments • Ear candy These elements may be

Custom Template dialog:

Custom Template ? ☒

Template: 5.1 Surround DVD ▼ 🖫 ✕

Description: Audio: 448 Kbps, 48,000 Hz, 5.1 Surround
Main Audio Service: Complete main
Use this setting for 5.1 Surround DVD soundtracks.

Audio service configuration

Bitstream mode: Main audio service: Complete main ▼

Audio coding mode: 3/2 (L, C, R, Ls, Rs) ▼ ☑ Enable LFE

Sample rate: 48 kHz ▼

Data rate: 448 kbps ▼ Audio bandwidth: 20.34 kHz

Dialog normalization: -27 dB ▼

☐ Save data in Intel byte order (LSB first)

DD DOLBY DIGITAL

Audio Service / Bitstream / Ext. Bitstream / Preprocessing

OK   Cancel

First, you need to find, record, or choose the best sound elements. Next, you must fix any problems and clean up the elements for the best possible fidelity. Then you can turn your attention to balancing the individual parts into a cohesive whole. This will include managing volume levels of all the tracks and often individual elements within a track. You'll also need to place all these sounds in the surround field.

The specific content will drive many creative decisions. For instance, you may need to use certain audio effects such as compression, equalization, and so forth to further refine the mix. There may be a need for other special audio effects to make the track more realistic and enjoyable. Finally, you'll need to master the final mix and encode it to the surround format your distribution media prefers, such as AC-3 for DVD.

Your surround sound authoring program should give you the control you need over volume, panning, and effects. The surround encoder provides settings for getting the best encode.

Soundcard Properties

Depending on your chosen soundcard, there may be some setup issues required such as assigning outputs to specific channels.

Additionally, you may need to set up how your surround authoring software communicates with the soundcard. This may be a function of your authoring application, the soundcard, or both. For example, choose the soundcard and assign which of its outputs carry the six channels.

If your soundcard has bass management, disable it at this point. This is useful only to check your mix on an alternate and optional consumer system that you may use in addition to your professional surround mixing environment. Bass management is not used when authoring surround.

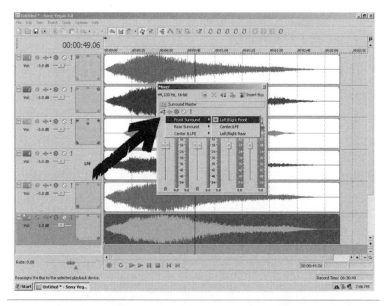

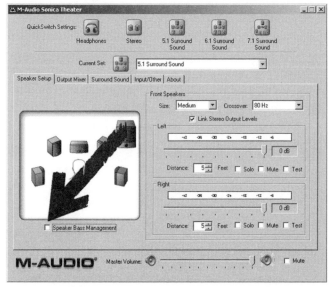

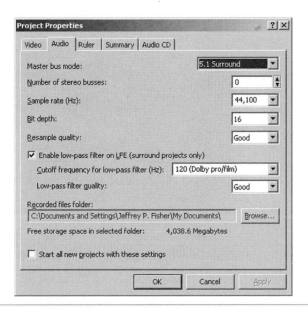

Project Properties

Again, your surround authoring program will have specific procedures for setting up a surround project. Access these properties and configure them accordingly. For example, the audio properties in Sony Vegas allow choosing either a stereo or 5.1 mixing environment.

Do not confuse the LFE low-pass with bass management; these are separate issues.

There may be additional settings for optimizing the surround project. You should enable the low-pass filter on the LFE and choose the cutoff frequency based on your specific surround sound needs. Typically, use 80Hz for DVD and 120Hz for film.

As you assign sounds to the LFE, this low-pass filter keeps out higher frequencies (above the cutoff point) and ensures that only deep bass content is sent to the LFE speaker.

Generic Functions

Each track in your authoring program should have its own volume level control. Use this to balance the loudness of sounds assigned to that track with the rest of your mix.

Each track also has a surround sound panning control. This allows positioning the sound in the surround field. The panner shows the speakers with an icon representing the source track. Click and drag the source icon to position the track as needed.

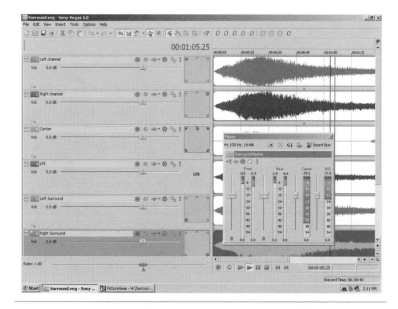

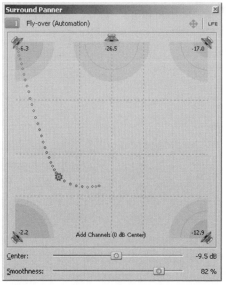

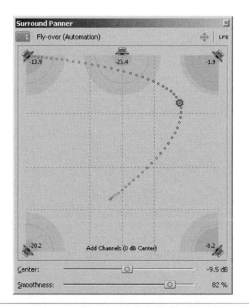

Notice the speaker's level changes as you move the track around.

Some surround panners offer greater control beyond simple positioning.

Use controls to turn on and off speakers for a track.

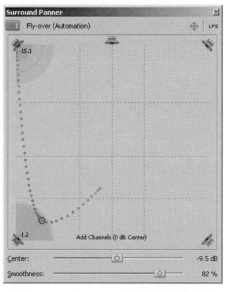

Adjust the level of the center channel in relation to the other speakers.

To keep a stereo source in its original stereo format, including its phantom center, position it at the front and either turn off the center or reduce its volume.

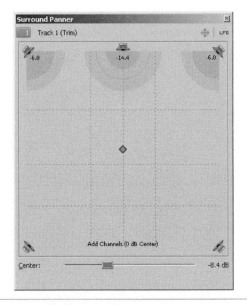

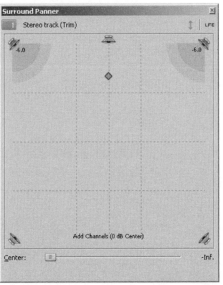

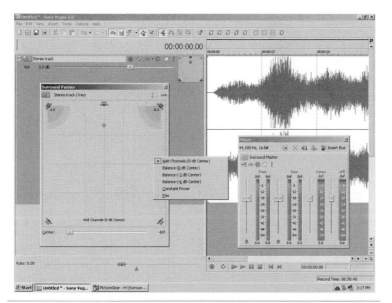

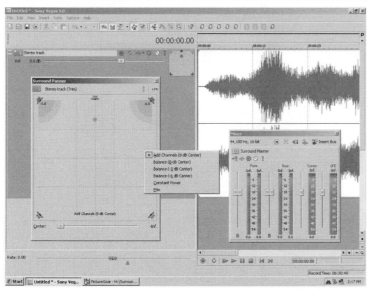

Select from a variety of panning modes that apply when panning stereo and mono sources:

- Add channels—combines channels as you pan. Watch for clipping (levels above 0dB).

- Balance (0, –3, –6 Center)—different settings determine how the center channel handles sounds as they pan toward and away from other speakers. Setting a maximum level minimizes clipping.

- Constant power—sounds keep their level as they pan. A good mode for mono sounds. This mode (or Film) is usually the best choice.

- Film—emulates the theatrical mixing environment and uses constant power.

Constrain movements to free, up, down, left, and right.

Assign a track to the LFE only.

The Surround Master Bus provides independent level controls for all six channels. Meters show the levels, too.

Add a file to a track and use that track's surround panner to move the file around as it plays. Watch the master bus to see how the level changes as the sound moves from speaker to speaker.

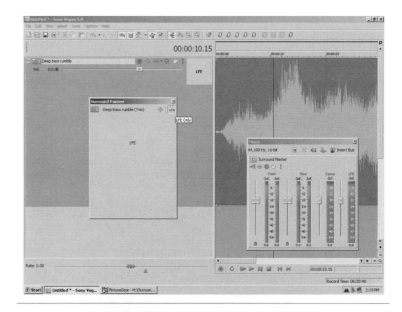

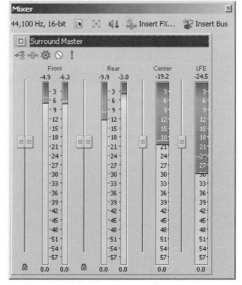

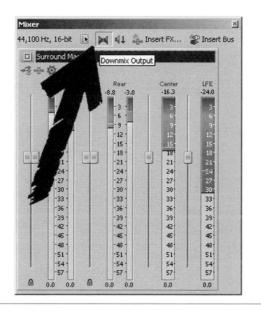

The Surround Master may also have a downmix button that lets you check the stereo compatibility of your project with the click of the mouse.

If you add additional buses, including assignable effects buses, they should have their own level controls and surround sound panners.

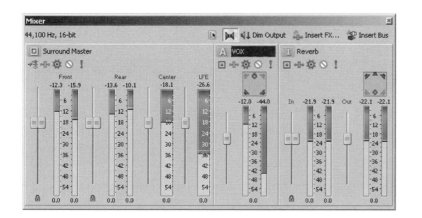

Buses are a mixer within the main mixer that enable combining multiple tracks to one level and pan control. For example, you may have several drum tracks (kick, snare, toms, cymbals, and overheads) giving you complete control over their sound. However, you could assign all those individual tracks to one bus for final level control and pan positioning.

Assignable effects allow sending multiple tracks to the same effect. For example, you could add reverb to just the snare, tom, and overhead tracks from the drum example above, leaving the kick dry. Plus, you could control how much of each track gets reverb, the overall amount of reverb on the track, and its positioning.

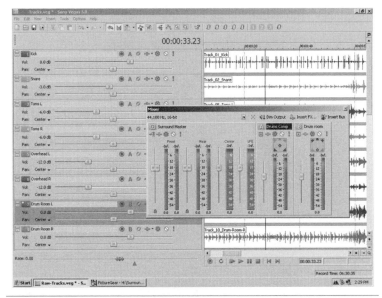

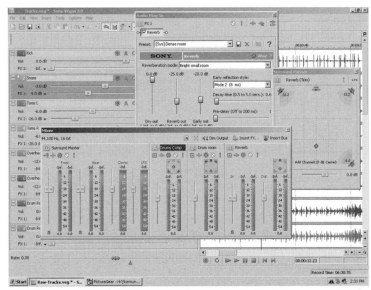

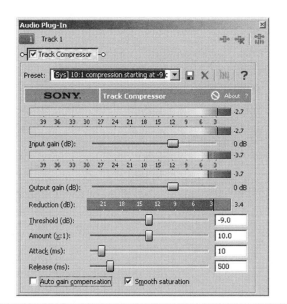

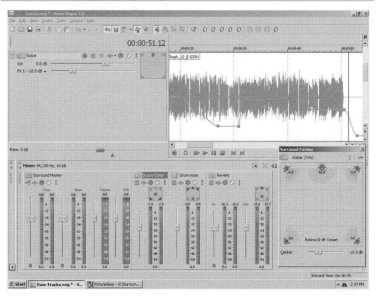

You may also be able to add effects at the track level. Effects added here apply to every sound element on the track. These effects are often non-destructive, meaning the original audio files are unaffected by any changes. Your audio software applies these effects in real time.

Automation

If your surround authoring program offers automation of levels and panning, your resulting mixes can be more dynamic and interesting. Software automation relies on break-point envelopes for controlling parameters. How the envelopes work varies by software.

- Manually—use the mouse to add nodes and drag envelope points to the desired levels and positions.

- Recording mode—use the mouse to manipulate faders, sliders, knobs, and buttons in real time as the file plays. The software records the moves and plays them back. The recorded envelopes can usually be edited, too.

- External hardware—uses a device that emulates a hardware mixer in both manual and recording modes.

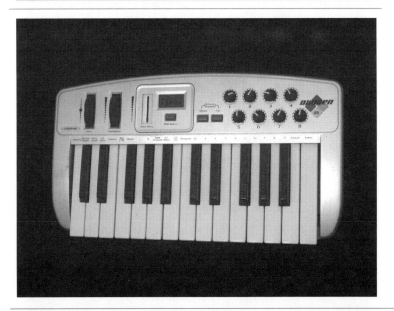

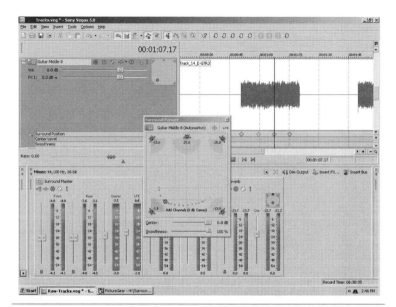

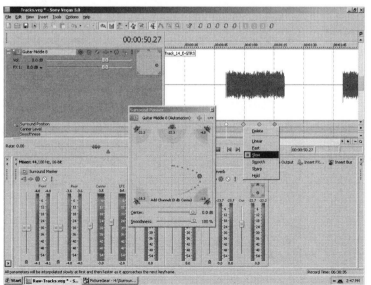

Alternately, the software may use keyframes for its automation. Keyframes are a reference to a specific point in time. The software then gradually changes settings based on these keyframes.

There are smoothness settings for determining how the program moves between keyframes, such as linear, fast, slow, smooth, and sharp.

Chapter 5

Bass Management, Center Channel, and Downmix

There are some crucial surround caveats that you must both understand and handle. This chapter addresses the details concerning the LFE and center channels along with the upshot on downmixing.

LFE and Subwoofer

As has been mentioned, it's important to note the difference between the LFE channel and the subwoofer. The sub is an actual physical component—a speaker designed to reproduce low frequencies. The LFE is a surround effects channel for carrying special low-frequency effects. The confusion comes from the fact that the LFE effects are actually reproduced by a subwoofer.

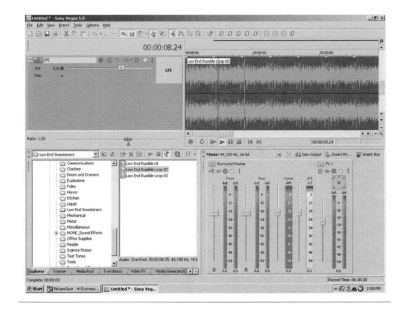

Unfortunately, many people mistakenly believe that the LFE is for all the bass in the project. This is untrue. The LFE is a dedicated, low-frequency enhancement channel reserved for certain sonic effects. The LFE does not extend the bass of the program material. On the contrary, the five main speakers are full-range.

The LFE simply provides more bass volume to compensate for our ear's reduced sensitivity of bass frequencies. These low frequency effects—explosions, rumbles, et al—are more felt than heard. In short, the LFE is best used to sweeten the bass and not function as the sole supplier of bass content.

Because of the LFE's role, keep all the bass content in the five main speakers. Let your LFE assignments be icing on the cake. If you use the LFE for more than effects, many listeners will not hear them, as some do not have speakers capable of effectively reproducing the LFE sounds. Additionally, the LFE is left out of the downmix equation (discussed below).

There's no way this tiny satellite speaker is going to reproduce any significant bass content.

Bass Management

Here's the real rub. In many consumer surround sound playback systems, the subwoofer has two functions. It, of course, carries the LFE channel information. It also carries the bass from the five main speakers, too. This is because many consumer surround sound systems use limited-bandwidth satellite speakers for the five main channels. These speakers do not extend far enough down into the low-frequency range; they lack bass. To compensate for the satellite's inability to reproduce low frequencies, bass sounds are routed to the system's subwoofer. This sub now provides all the bass, including the LFE. This process is called bass management.

If you are following the advice in this book, your LCR/LsRs monitors are full-range and there is no bass management involved. This is the proper way to mix. However, you still need to be aware of how bass management affects your surround sound mixes. If you supply too much bass in the mains plus LFE content, the finished mix could overtax the subwoofer in a bass-managed system.

There are no hard and fast rules. However, keeping an eye on the LFE levels and factoring the amount of bass content in your project are important considerations. This fact is why I recommend testing your mixes on a consumer bass-managed system. Experience will dictate the right approach and how far you can push the bass. Until you get that experience, test!

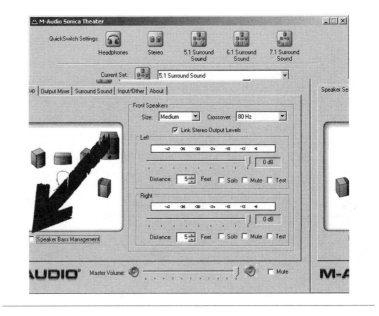

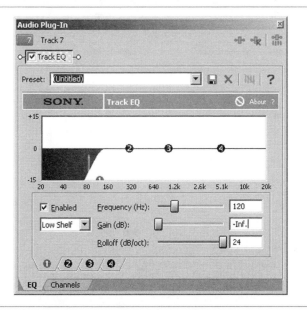

LFE and Content

The LFE is designed only for low-frequency sounds; therefore it is best to limit the bandwidth of the sounds you assign to the LFE. Some authoring programs give you control over what gets sent to the LFE. The project properties page in Sony Vegas, for example, lets you choose the LFE low-pass filter cutoff.

If your software does not offer this, apply a low-pass filter to each track sent to the LFE. This low-pass filter can range between 80Hz and 120Hz. Use a steep filter, 24dB per octave.

The Dolby AC-3 encoder can additionally apply the LFE low-pass filter to further ensure that high frequencies are not present in that channel.

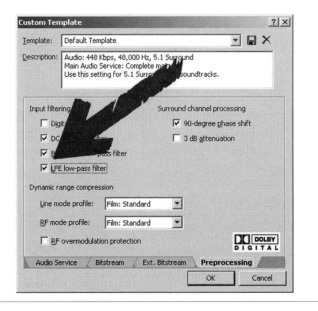

Downmixing the 5.1 project to stereo (or mono) ignores the LFE content.

For music-only projects, use of the LFE is up for debate. Because the bass content should be in the main five speakers, there is merit to ignoring the LFE entirely. Contrarily, music mixers are starting to take advantage of the LFE's extra "umph." This gives a little extra ear candy for listeners with better playback systems. Proceed with caution, though. This approach is best used to enhance the music above and beyond a solid overall balance in the five mains. Remember this as you plan what goes to the LFE.

For audio post projects, the LFE is used to support the content when applicable. For dramatic presentations, these low-frequency effects can contribute to the audience's enjoyment. If you are film mixing, judicious use of the LFE can add to the sonic illusion of the presentation. The use of the LFE varies by content, though. For a corporate documentary or wedding event, the need for the LFE is significantly diminished, if necessary at all.

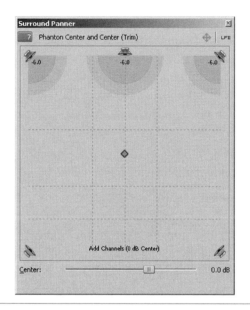

Center Caveats

The dedicated center channel also has some issues worth exploring. Its purpose was originally intended to anchor dialog to the center of the movie theater screen. No matter where the audience sat in the theater, the dialog came from the screen. This convention has extended to TV as well. Coupled to the center channel is the phantom center created by the stereo front left and right channels. Therefore, there are technically two centers that you must balance.

The best tactic is to avoid the either/or mentality. For any sound assigned to the center channel, mix some of it to the stereo phantom center, too. This is important for the downmix, too, as will be discussed below.

For music-only mixes, the center channel can be used for centered sound elements, such as lead vocals, bass, kick drum, and other lead instruments. However, many surround mixers avoid the center channel completely (and the LFE for that matter) and instead rely on the front L/R and surround speakers only. This effectively turns 5.1 mixes into 4.0 mixes. This decision to avoid the center channel was often based on a misunderstanding of its purpose.

Some early surround mixers placed the lead vocal in the center channel in its most naked form usually without effects. Any effects, such as reverb and delay were then added to the stereo L/R front speakers. Listeners discovered this and started unplugging speakers and listening to the *a cappella* vocal alone. Any imperfections on the vocal track became glaringly obvious in this configuration. Subsequently, news of this tactic scared many surround sound music mixers away from the center channel.

Keep in mind that with music mixes, the center channel functions as an enhancement channel. To reiterate, any sound element assigned to the center should also be in the stereo phantom center. I'd suggest putting most in the stereo center and just a little in the dedicated center channel. Also, don't fall prey to putting just dry (without effects) sounds in the center. Treat the center as you would any of the other speakers.

For audio post projects, the center channel reverts to its fundamental role: the place for the dialog. It is film and TV convention to center the dialog even if the on-screen characters are positioned to one side of the screen. And although an off-camera voice can be panned to one side (or even to the surrounds), on-camera dialog and voice-over are best placed in the center channel. Again, sending a little center channel to the front stereo L/R channels is good practice, too.

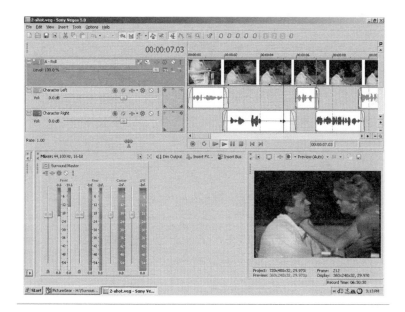

Here's why: Picture two actors sitting across from one another in a two-shot. You could pan the actors according to their position; left actor in left speaker, right actor in the right speaker. Next, the editing cuts to a close-up of the left actor. You'd have to pan the sound to the center to match the shot. The editing cuts back to the two-shot, and the voice would pan away from center. The audience will be distracted by this approach as dialog appears to jump around the room. Avoid this situation or use it sparingly for a disorienting or otherwise creative effect.

Also note, that many consumer surround systems use an inferior center channel speaker, often with reduced bandwidth. The center may be optimized for dialog only, which could have adverse effects on other content placed in the center channel. Not to harp on this point too much, but ... you need to test your mixes on a variety of consumer systems whenever you can.

Don't tell anybody I told you this, but try taking a mix to your local electronics superstore and test it on all the systems they have on display. Keep on testing until they ask you to leave!

Phantom Ghosts

Though there is a strong phantom center between the stereo front speakers that is reinforced via the center channel's contribution, the same is not true of the other stereo "pairs." The phantom images formed between the L/Ls and R/Rs are not so pronounced or distinct. Neither is the phantom center formed between the Ls/Rs speakers as easy to perceive.

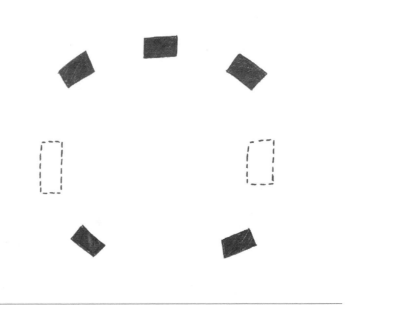

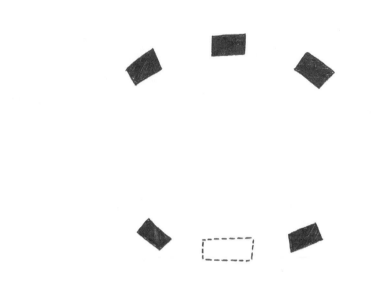

The primary reason for this discrepancy is due to our specific physical make-up. Our ears are separated by a large object—our head!—and that means sounds arriving from the side and back arrive in our ears at different times. The resulting phase shift makes them sound different. Our brain uses this information to pinpoint direction. There are even mathematical formulas, called head-related transfer functions (HRTF) that can predict these changes.

Suffice to say that it is harder for us to localize sounds placed in these areas, and each movement of our head seems to affect where they appear to be, too. So, while surround sound provides envelopment, it does lack distinct localization on the sides and back. Even if you place a sound to the right of your audience halfway between the front and back, they will be unable to pinpoint that direction accurately. They'll just know it's not coming from directly in front of them (and feel it's mostly behind or around them).

Because of HRTF, there is talk of expanding the surround format with more speakers in front, to the side and rear, and even overhead to balance envelopment with distinct sound localization. For example, the Dolby EX format (6.1) adds a center channel to the surrounds to overcome this limitation somewhat.

Another proposal is for a 10.2 standard with five front speakers: L, LC, C, RC, R, three surrounds: LsCsRs, two side fills: L/R, and stereo LFE channels. I'm not sure television viewing rooms across the world are ready for 12 speakers, though!

Another aspect of HRTF is that the frequency response of our ears to sounds coming from the rear is different. Any sound element assigned exclusively to the rear will sound different than the same sound assigned solely to the front. There's nothing wrong with your hearing (or your speakers); it's just your head getting in the way.

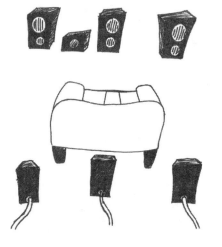

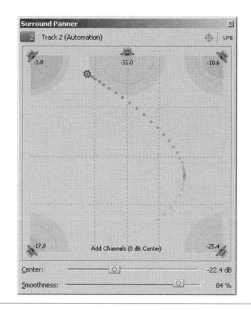

Be aware of this if you dynamically pan sounds from front to back and vice versa. The quality of the sound may change noticeably. To a certain extent, such as a spaceship flyover in a movie, the shift contributes to the effect. We are conditioned to hear the change from behind to in front of us. For a music "flyover" the effect may be more pronounced, necessitating some compensation with tonal, EQ treatment.

Exit Sign Effect

Another issue to be concerned with is the so-called exit sign effect. Essentially, this entails moving a sound element in such a way that people look away from the screen (at the theater exit sign presumably) to follow the sound. For music, a sound event may also pull attention away from the overall mix to a distinct sound in a channel. These results may or may not be desirable.

Downmix Nixes

If the playback system is not 5.1 com-
patible, the surround sound decoder
collapses, or downmixes, the six channels to two stereo channels (or even
mono). What happens to the dedicated
center, surround, and LFE information?
During the encode you can specify
how the decoder handles these channels.

Typically, both the center and surround channels are turned down, or
attenuated, by 3dB. This ensures an
acceptable balance when added to the
conventional L/R stereo. However, the
LFE content is completely ignored.
This means that anybody who listens
to your 5.1 mix using only a stereo
playback arrangement will *not* hear
any of sounds that were routed to the
LFE. This is yet another reason to use
the LFE with caution.

There are actually two downmix options

- Lo/Ro—The center channel gets added to the front L/R and the surrounds are added to their respective front channels (Ls to L and Rs to R). This is the most common arrangement.

- Lt/Rt—The center channel is added to the front L/R channels. The decoder then sums the surround channels (to mono) and adds them to both the left and right channels with the right 90 degrees out of phase. This format allows a Dolby Pro Logic decoder to reproduce its LCRS signal for those using such a system.

When encoding to AC-3, you can set metadata parameters to direct how the decoder downmixes your content. These options will be discussed further in the encoding chapter.

Maintaining compatibility with Dolby Pro Logic is another downmix issue. Because the Pro Logic encoder uses a phase-based matrix, some 5.1 material may "confuse" the encoder or decoder resulting in incorrect steering issues. For example, musical instruments with a phasing effect (a sort of swirling sound) can create unpredictable results when played back in the LCRS environment. The sound may jump around the room. Also, some stereo micing techniques, such as XY can fool the Pro Logic system, too.

With discrete Dolby Digital 5.1, these issues can be ignored. However, there is a large base of Pro Logic gear in living rooms, so these problems will not go away soon.

Surround Downmix Issues

As was mentioned earlier, film surround sound mixers often calibrate their surround speakers 3dB lower to emulate typical theater arrangements. Rear surround channels in U.S. theaters are calibrated to 82dB, while the front reference is 85dB. However, consumers reference the same level for all five speakers. This means the surrounds will be 3dB louder when a theatrical mix is played in the home. To compensate, the encoder supports attenuating the surrounds by 3dB. TV mixers also often attenuate the surrounds by 3dB at the encoding step. This is to compensate for the fact that listeners frequently sit closer to the surround speakers in many homes.

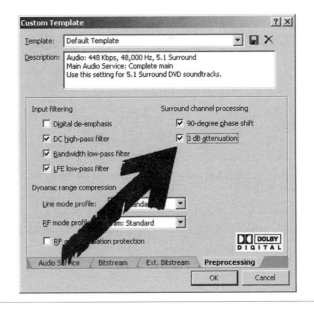

Separate 5.1 and Stereo Is Best

What should be obvious is that down-mixing, and to a certain extent bass management, affects how your mix sounds in different playback environments. Although you can direct what the decoder does in certain instances, you can't be completely sure. For the best results, I recommend you do a separate stereo mix of all your 5.1 projects and include that for listeners to choose if they lack a surround sound playback system. Having two separate mixes is the only sure-fire way to be sure that listeners hear what you intend.

Chapter 6

Music Surround Mixing Tips

If you've struggled making your mono and stereo music mixes sound their best, you may find surround sound surprisingly easier to work with. Sound engineers always complain about how hard it is to balance disparate elements into a coherent mix.

Surround lets you literally move problem sounds out of the way. Many mixers comment on how there is a reduced need for compression and how radical EQ is so important to stereo mixing. The 360-degree sound field gives a wider and deeper stage for placing sound elements. The result is a more open and natural mix free from the over-processing required by stereo mixing.

The Rules

Early surround music mixes used the Ls/Rs primarily for ambience and effects. Today, the trend is toward immersing the listener *in* the music. Gone are gimmicks of panning sounds around the room, gimmicks which have thankfully been replaced with judicious use of all six speakers. All of this adds up to one simple point:

There are no rules when mixing music in surround!

You are free to experiment with what you feel best presents the music. This doesn't mean you should ignore the points presented earlier. On the contrary, you must fully understand all the caveats so that your mixes translate well to a variety of playback systems.

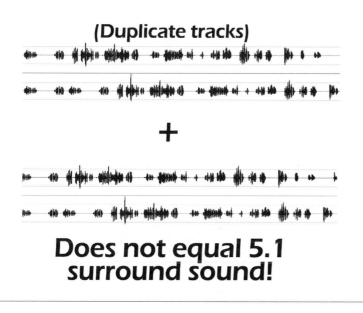

(Duplicate tracks)

+

Does not equal 5.1 surround sound!

The Case Against Surround Upmixing

There is an emerging trend of reissuing popular albums in 5.1. In most cases, there is access to the original multitrack masters. This means all the original parts can be rebalanced into an original mix designed exclusively for surround playback.

Unfortunately, there are a few recordings that no longer exist as multitracks. Creating a faux surround mix from a mono or stereo source, called upmixing, is quite simple. That doesn't mean it is the right thing to do. In fact, the Recording Academy expressly prohibits surround upmixing.

If you are working with your own music compositions or other multitrack masters, upmixing will not be an issue. If you are asked to create an upmix from a stereo recording, you may want to attach a disclaimer to the finished recording.

Correlated vs. Decorrelated

If you use the same sounds and effects in many channels (such as L/R and Ls/Rs), the parts sum together with a more monaural result. In short, the more the channels are alike, the more monaural and less pronounced the surround effect. In this example, the sounds and effects are said to be correlated.

For a bigger and better surround experience, use sounds and effects that are decorrelated or different. For example, when you assign the same sound to different channels, adjust the EQ, pitch, delay, and reverb settings so the sound is distinct in each channel. Similarly, use two mono reverbs with different settings instead of one stereo reverb. These subtle changes greatly enhance the surround effect.

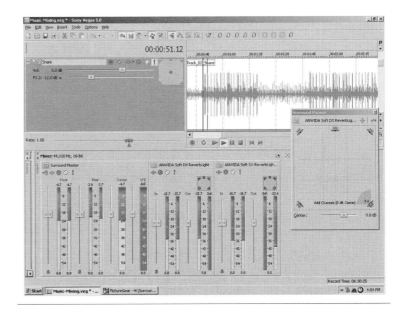

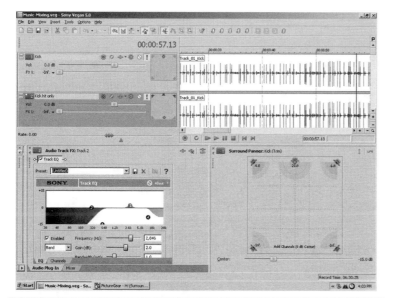

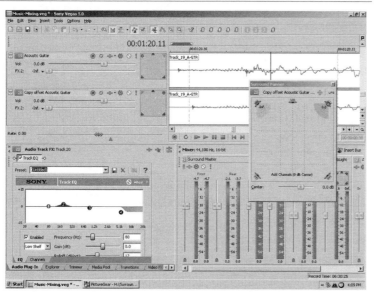

Another way to decorrelate sounds is to split their frequency spectrum to different channels. For example, the bass drum has both high- and low-frequency components. The mallet striking the head is higher in pitch than the resonant tone of the drum itself. You could, for instance, route the percussive attack to the surrounds and the boom to the front for a unique effect.

Short time delays also decorrelate and open up the sound. For example, duplicate an acoustic guitar part and offset the duplicated track slightly in time. Pan the two parts to opposite channels, say front L and R, respectively. The guitar part spreads out across the entire front, leaving a nice hole in the center for a vocal part to sit. Boosting the bass EQ a little on one side and the highs moderately on the duplicate can enhance the effect as can adding a slight chorus to one part only.

Using Surround Recordings

If you are fortunate to have some discrete surround recordings, bringing them into your project is straightforward. Add the individual parts to the Timeline and use the surround panner to position them. Assign the channels to match their original recording position and turn off all other speakers for that track.

Before You Mix

With rare exceptions, most music today is recorded using multitracking. Each part is carefully recorded and isolated from the other sounds. Engineers strive to record a clean, loud, and dry sound. This approach gives the engineer, and later the mixer, complete control over how each element sounds. Sometimes multiple parts are recorded at once, but more often parts are recorded separately and individually, even days, months, or years apart. The majority of parts are recorded monaural with little or no room ambience, too.

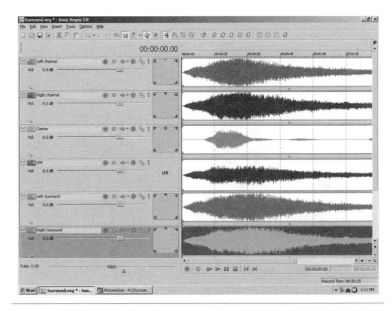

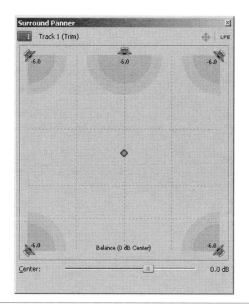

Once everything is recorded, the task is to combine all these parts into a finished whole. Mixing adds effects and artificial ambience to the multitrack parts. Engineers work hard to balance volume, frequencies, and position. Ironically, the point is to make the musicians sound as if they all played the music together in a room.

Surround sound mixing opens up additional possibilities. Even with most sounds originating in mono, there are unique techniques for creating an interesting surround experience. First, you must answer these questions:

- Do you want your listener in the room with the musicians?

- Or do you want your musicians playing in front of the listener?

The former entails immersing your listeners *in* the recording while the latter is a more traditional audience perspective—the musicians are on stage and the listener is in the audience.

Increasingly, surround music projects are taking the in-the-band perspective. The audience perspective has been relegated to live recordings, where room ambience and audience noise can be presented in the surrounds.

Surround-izing

Building realistic ambiences around mono (and stereo) music parts calls for both surround positioning and time-based effects (delay, reverb). There are two methods for creating surround from these sources:

- Surround positioning

- Effects in opposite channels

Simply moving a mono or stereo source using the surround sound panner to a different location can open up the sound, making it appear more in or around the room.

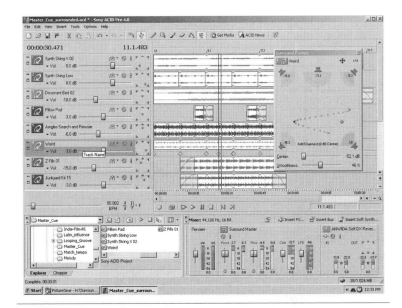

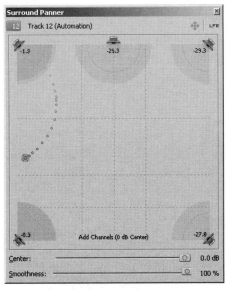

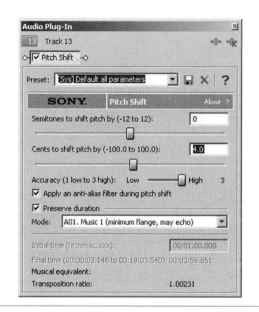

Using effects is another method. Effects can be divided into several categories.

- Tonal-based effects, such as EQ, work on the frequency content of the audio.

- Time-based effects, such as reverb and delay, give a sense of space, such as the sound of a room, or add discreet repeats or echoes to the sound.

- Modulation-based effects, such as flange, chorus, and phase, are time-based effects that include modulation or resonance settings that change the effect over time.

- Dynamics-based effects, essentially compression, reduce the dynamic range of an audio file.

- Pitch-based effects alter the original frequency of a file.

Effects make it easier to decorrelate sounds. For example, duplicate a mono sound, EQ one differently, and then pan them to different locations. Slight pitch differences, just a few cents, between channels can make a sound appear bigger, too.

By far the easiest way to surround-ize a sound is to use delay or reverb or both. Position a sound in the front speakers. Use an effects send to tap off some of the signal and route the output of that to the surrounds. Two separate mono reverbs or delays with unique settings can enhance the effect.

Place a stereo multitap delay in the rears. Set it up to ping-pong back and forth between the two speakers with each delay. Feed a little of a vocal or instrument solo to it. The part will mostly be in the front with the repeat echoes bouncing around in the rear.

In Their Face

Here's how to place a sound right in the listener's face. Balance the sound, say a lead guitar solo, in the center channel with the two rear surrounds. Turn off the other speakers. Use the surround panner until the solo is right in your face while mixing. For the rears, add a slight pitch, delay, or phase shift. Play with the balance and discover how to place sounds over a shoulder and other areas behind and to the side.

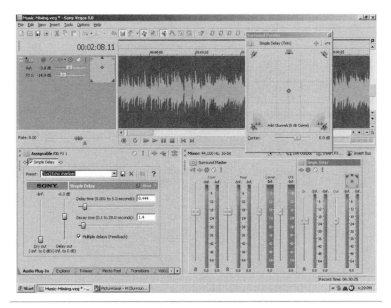

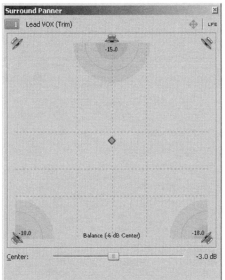

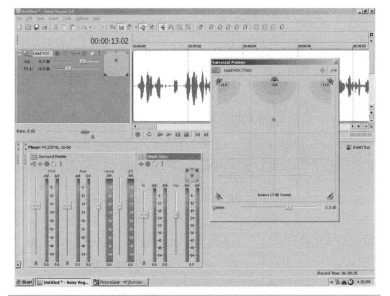

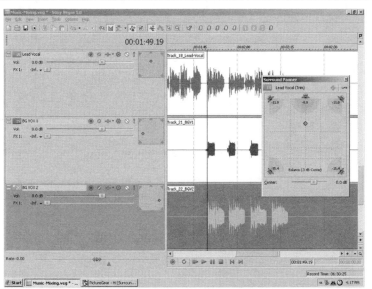

Vocals

Make sure your vocals can be heard and understood clearly. Place lead vocals typically in the center of a traditional music mix. Vocals benefit from both center channel and stereo phantom placement; put a little of the vocal in both. Do be aware that a vocal in the phantom center can "move" in relation to the same vocal anchored in the center channel depending on where the listener is. Avoid the dead-dry vocal routed exclusively to the center channel speaker; put some light effects in the center channel along with it.

Place the singer's breath only in the rears, the words in the front center. This way the voice slides forward gently on every breath.

Place harmony and other background vocals "around" the lead vocal. For example, the lead vocal could move toward the listener while the background parts fill in behind and around the lead. A choir might work exclusively in the surrounds with some reverb in the front L/R.

Double-track a vocal. Place one in the center and the other in the phantom center. Alternately, place the first vocal as you like. Route the second vocal take to reverb only and have the reverb play in the surrounds only.

Drums

If you're fortunate to have individual drums isolated on their own channels, you have a little more control over your surround mix. If you only have a stereo drum part, your choices are limited. Typically, the rule is to center the bass drum, or kick drum, and the snare. Place toms and cymbals depending on the perspective you want to achieve. You could, for instance, place the listener in the drummer's perspective behind the kit or the audience's perspective in front of the drum kit.

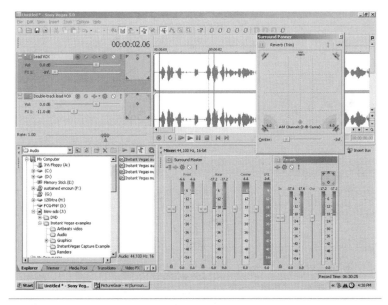

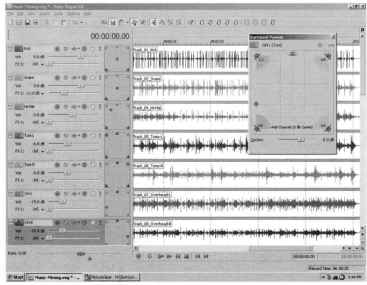

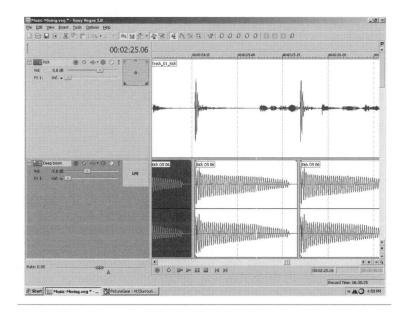

Again, avoid the center channel only with centered drums such as the kick or snare. Place them in both the phantom and dedicated center channels. Also, don't be tempted to route the kick exclusively to the LFE for reasons mentioned earlier in this book. You might, however, duplicate the kick part or use an alternate deep bass sound and route that to the LFE for extra punch.

Remember HRTF: the surrounds sound different than the front!

Percussive elements may work well with more dramatic surround positioning, too. These choices depend on the song and the goals you want to achieve with your mix. Don't be afraid to experiment, but do learn to balance effects with tricks that may distract your listeners.

Bass

The bass is the low-end anchor for most music projects. Typically, place it in the center, leaning more toward the L/R phantom center than the dedicated center channel. Our ears do not localize bass frequencies well, so precise positioning is unnecessary. Duplicating the bass part or using another recording and routing it to the LFE can be acceptable.

Rhythm Instruments

Rhythm instruments typically support the lead vocals and provide the melodic content missing from the unpitched percussion. Keeping these parts out of the phantom and dedicated centers is a good idea.

Often hard-panning rhythm parts creates a bigger sound that is more open. For example, place the rhythm guitar to the left and the rhythm piano to the right.

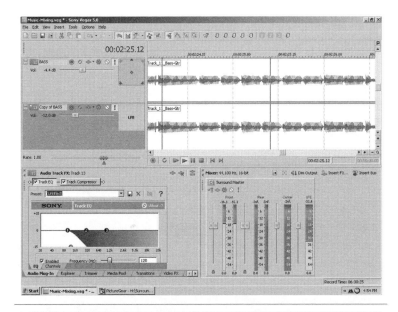

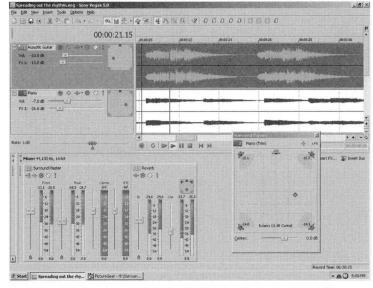

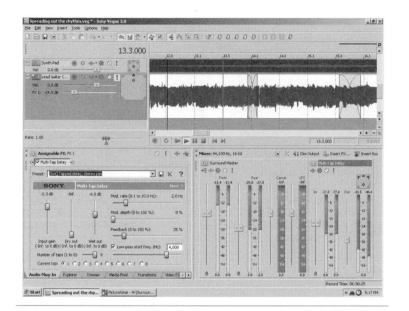

Lead Instruments

Much like lead vocals, lead instruments deserve special attention. It is common practice for a lead part, such as a guitar solo, to take the place of the lead vocal during its section of the song. That may or may not be the best approach. The lead section might call for aggressive use of surround. For example, it might start behind the listener and then take center stage or vice-versa. Alternately, placing a delay in the Ls/Rs can appear to have the notes sail over the listener or even bounce around the room.

Place the initial attack of a guitar part in the rears and then the full-quality guitar solo in stereo in the front.

Ear Candy

You have six speakers at your disposal to place the big and subtle elements that make a song interesting to hear. Get creative!

Going into or coming from a song chorus is a good place for some surround ear candy.

Dynamic Panning

Music balances repetition with change. Your mix should do the same.

The choice to include surround sound panning in your music mix is up to you. While having the 360-degree sound field makes placing individual musical parts around the listener easier, moving those parts around *during* the mix may not work. In general, subtle panning is probably better than constant movement. That said, one big flourish where everything seems to change positions at once might be an unexpected surprise for the listener.

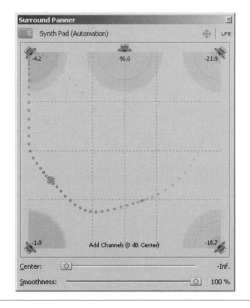

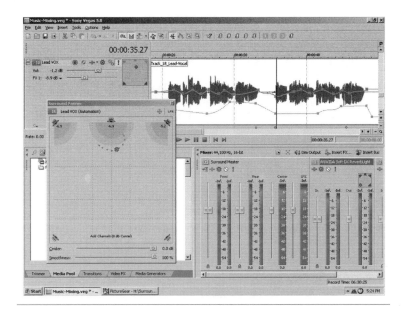

That said, I feel that movement is the key to a great-sounding mix, whether mono, stereo, or 5.1. I'm constantly tweaking volume and pan position on my mixes in an attempt to create a more vibrant mix. I'm talking subtle changes here, not having the drums panning around the room like *In-A-Gadda-Da-Vida*. I also recommend changing effects, too, for example, adding a little more reverb here, a little less there. If your mixing software lets you automate these parameters, the mix can be far stronger.

Mastering surround may seem difficult at first; ultimately, it's a more flexible, powerful and sometimes easier way to mix your projects.

Multitrack Music Mixing in Action

Crafting a cohesive surround sound music mix from disparate musical elements is a challenge. It is also a lot of fun tweaking parameters until the finished mix emerges. Let's bring the ideas discussed in this chapter and throughout the book together and work through a mix step by step.

There is one caveat, though. The choices you make depend entirely on the goals of your project. They also depend on the music itself and the demands of that material. This section offers ideas and possibilities. It's up to you to apply them to your projects.

This rock song was recorded using traditional multitrack methods. Several mics were used to pick up the individual drums and either routed to individual tracks or mixed into composites. The bass and clean guitar were recorded dry using a direct box. The distorted guitars and solos used various amp and mic combinations. Vocals, lead and harmony, were recorded last.

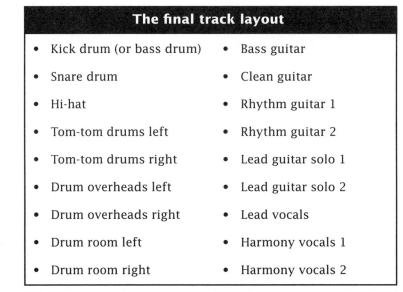

The final track layout	
• Kick drum (or bass drum)	• Bass guitar
• Snare drum	• Clean guitar
• Hi-hat	• Rhythm guitar 1
• Tom-tom drums left	• Rhythm guitar 2
• Tom-tom drums right	• Lead guitar solo 1
• Drum overheads left	• Lead guitar solo 2
• Drum overheads right	• Lead vocals
• Drum room left	• Harmony vocals 1
• Drum room right	• Harmony vocals 2

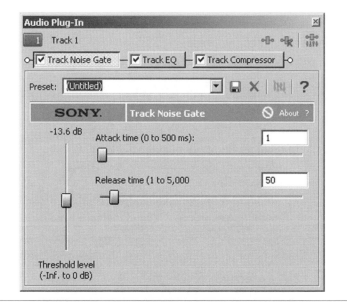

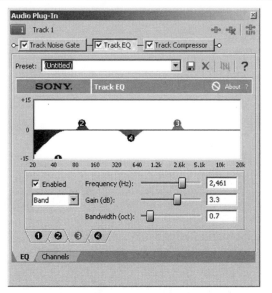

The drums are a crucial element of any pop or rock music mix, and this project is no exception. Focus on the kick drum first. There is some leakage of the other drums into this mic. Applying a noise gate and carefully setting the threshold effectively isolates the kick and eliminates the other sounds that the mic picked up.

Apply some compression (4:1, slow attack, fast release) to make the kick punchy. EQ to bring out the thump (+2db to 4dB at 100Hz), accentuate the snap (+2db to 4dB at 2,250Hz), and thin the mud (–3db to 5dB between 400–600Hz).

Isolate the snare by using another noise gate on its track. Use slightly more aggressive compression (6:1 to 8:1, very slow attack, slow release), and EQ to taste: crack at 1,250Hz, crispness at 5,500Hz. Check it with the kick to make sure they sound right together.

Isolating the hi-hat is somewhat more difficult because if it's a busy pattern, gating it sounds choppy. To solve this problem, use EQ to thin out the drums that bleed. Try a shelving EQ and roll off all frequencies below 800Hz—higher if the cymbal still sounds satisfactory. Add some air to the cymbal with an EQ boost between 8,000–10,000Hz.

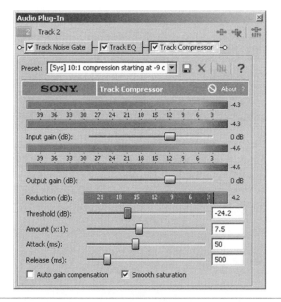

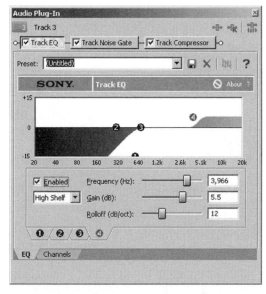

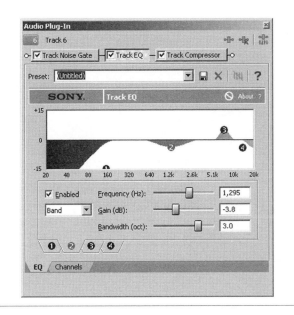

Gate the toms, add some compression, and tweak the EQ until they sit in the mix and don't fight for attention with the combination of kick and snare. Depending on what the drummer plays, you may need to be more aggressive with EQ here.

What's really important is the overall mix, not how each instrument sounds.

Be careful not to tweak individual parts too much. You may find that you get a killer sound when a single instrument or track is soloed. Unfortunately, the overall mix may not work. Don't worry about how something sounds completely on its own. Focus on the big picture. If it sounds right in the mix, it's right. Trust your ears.

Overheads usually grab the cymbals and the sound of the kit as a whole. EQ and compression can let you accentuate one or the other, typically not both, though.

Surround positions for these tracks is fairly straightforward. Put the kick to the center, snare slightly to one side, and hi-hat further to that same side. Put the toms and overheads in their original stereo arrangement. Balance the volume levels for a good blend.

Balance the drum room mics accordingly. I often roll off the extreme lows and highs to thin their sound somewhat (but that depends on the "sound" of the room). Position these more toward their respective rear surrounds for a bigger drum sound.

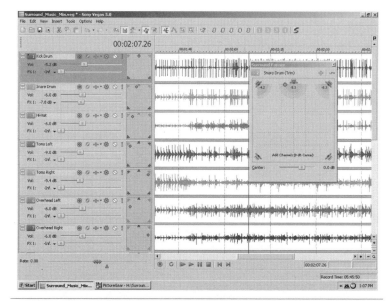

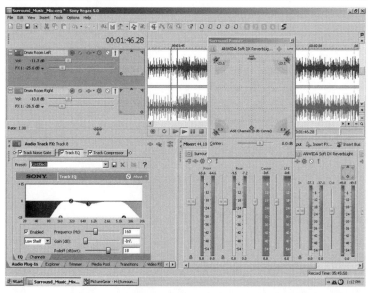

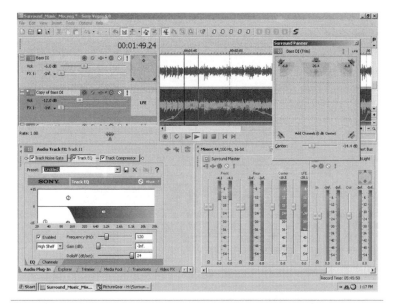

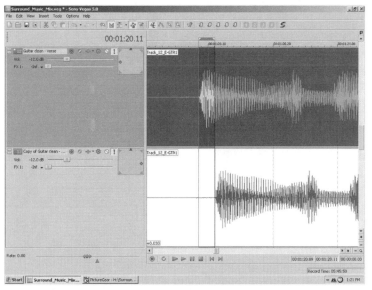

The bass guitar goes center of the stereo image, keeping most of it out of the dedicated center speaker. Duplicate the bass part, EQ out everything above 120Hz, limit it hard, and assign this copy to the LFE. Sneak this part in when it makes sense (such as during the chorus or guitar solo) by using volume automation.

The clean guitar part carries the chords of the song. Duplicate this track and offset the copy slightly in time. Hard-pan them left and right, respectively, and a little back into the room. Adjust volume so that it does not fight with the vocals.

Guitar 1 and 2 play in unison but sound distinctly different ('cos of different guitar, amp, and mic combinations). Put these two in the identical surround sound positions as the two clean guitar parts. Add a little chorus or slight pitch shift to one part for a bigger, more open sound. They often benefit from some bite with EQ boosts in the 8,000Hz area and mud relief by cutting the 400–800Hz range.

Place the guitar solos in the listener's face. Balance them using the center and L/R surrounds (turn off the front L/R speakers).

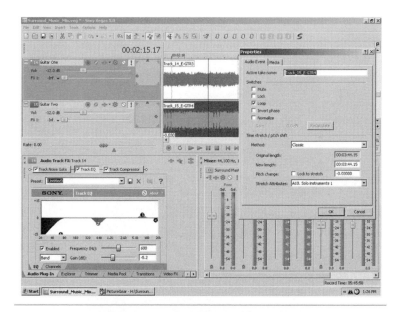

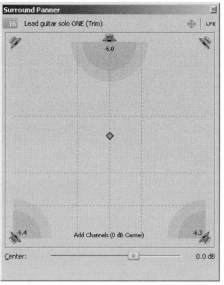

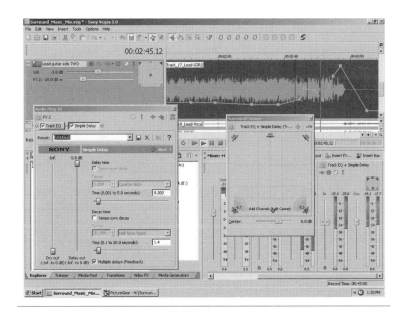

Add an insert effect with delay and assign it to the rear surrounds only. This way the guitar note echoes supplied by the delay sail over the audience to the rear. Tweak to really bring this effect out at critical musical sections, such as at the end of a phrase.

Make sure listeners can understand all the words being sung!

The quality of the vocal is often what people remember about a song. Take extreme care to present this performance in its best light. Always remember that people want to understand all the words. After hearing a song so many times, you get too familiar with it. The result is a tendency to push the vocals back into the mix too far. Fight that temptation!

Vocal EQ settings depend on too many factors. Generally, add some warmth with boosts in the 160Hz area for males and 320Hz for females. Take the mud out with cuts in the 400–700Hz range. Diction improves (as does speech intelligibility) in with boosts at 1,750Hz or 3,500Hz. Watch out for excessive S-sounds or sibilance though. Air is in the 8,000Hz range. Compression on the vocal can help it cut through a busy mix, too. Try between 3:1 to 5:1 with a fast attack and slow release.

Place the vocal in the front stereo L/R and the center. Any effects should be there, too. A nice lush reverb or a slap delay are good choices. I often use a delayed reverb by either tweaking its pre-delay setting or placing a delay effect before the reverb. This keeps the vocal mostly dry and up front in the mix with just the hint of reverb later—great for ballads!

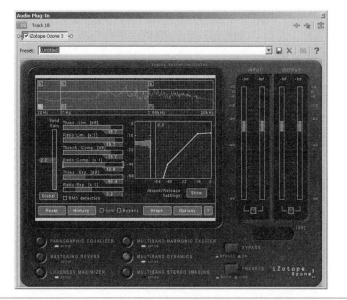

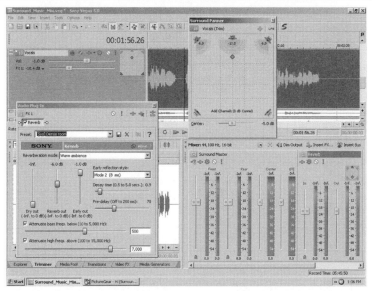

When using delays with music, it is desirable to match the repeats and echoes to the song tempo. A handy tool for figuring out the correct delay times based on tempo and note values is the free Delay Time Calculator software available from Analogx (www.analogx.com). They also offer other nifty (and free) software and Direct-X plug-ins.

Panning one harmony vocal to the left and the other to the right complements the lead vocal nicely. Duplicating the tracks, treating them with different EQ, effects, and even a slight pitch shift, and then positioning them all around the surround field can work to create a choir effect, too.

AnalogX Delay Time Calculator (www.analogx.com)

Tempo	2x Whole	Whole	Half	Quarter	Eighth	Sixteenth	Thirtysecond
132	909.091	454.545	227.273	113.636	56.818	28.409	14.205
Triplets	606.061	303.030	151.515	75.758	37.879	18.939	9.470

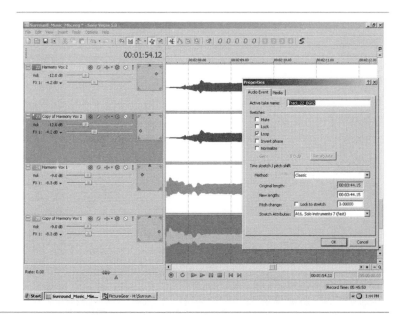

As final sweeteners, use some dynamic panning to add some movement to the mix. Don't go overboard. Just move some things around with the rhythm of the song. I often put my hands on the automation controls and "play" the song by moving volume, pan, and effects settings as the song plays. With the computer you can do multiple passes and even go back and fix mistakes.

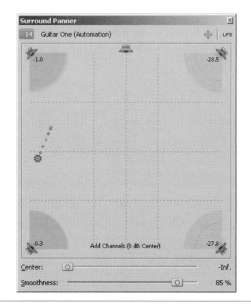

Chapter 7

Audio Post Surround Mixing Techniques

The soundtrack to any visual presentation is well over half the experience. Don't believe me? Put in your favorite Hollywood movie and watch it without the sound. While the visual aspects may still be stunning, it is the soundtrack that makes it all come alive. Building a surround sound mix to accompany your videos opens up a whole new world of creative expression. By far the easiest (and cheapest!) way to make your videos look better is to make them sound better.

Crafting the Killer Soundtrack

Most people mistakenly believe that the primary function of a soundtrack is to support the visual portion. Soundtracks create reality where none may exist. While that is very important, it's not always what is really going on. Good soundtracks play to the subtext of the piece and work their magic by directing audience attention and influencing emotion.

Audiences put up with "bad" video, but never poor sound.

Hold a "spotting" session with the director, picture editor, and producer to go through the video and discuss sound issues.

Whether you are working in video, TV, film, or games, the workflow for pulling together the soundtrack is deceptively simple:

1. Make decisions about all the sounds needed for the project. What do you have already and what do you need?

2. Gather all the sounds. This entails recording, creating them from scratch, layering, and drawing on pre-existing elements (such as sound effects libraries).

3. Tweak these sound elements to fit the project.

4. Synchronize the sounds to match on-screen action.

5. Mix the elements appropriately. Good soundtracks use contrast, volume, dynamics, surround placement, and effects appropriately, filling the sound frequency spectrum with deep lows, solid midrange, and crisp highs. You must juggle all the disparate sound elements, making speech intelligibility your number-one priority.

6. Deliver the completed soundtrack.

Soundtrack Elements Include:

Dialog

- Production dialog—includes interviews, stand-ups, etc.

- ADR "looped" dialog—fixed in post-production

- Group walla—post-recorded crowd sounds such as all the extras in a restaurant scene

- Voice-over

Sound Effects and Sound Design

- Production effects—field-recorded sounds

- Hard effects—typically post-synced sound effects such as a door closing

- Backgrounds—general sounds of places and settings, such as a factory

Foley

- Footsteps—recorded in post while watching the visuals and mimicking the action

- Clothing

- Props

Music

- Source—music seen and heard on screen, such as a radio playing

- Underscore—dramatic music

Sound Resources

There are many companies that offer buy-out sound effects and music on CD.

Sound Effects Libraries:

- Hollywood Edge (www.hollywoodedge.com)

- Sonomic (www.sonomic.com)

- SoundDogs.com (www.sounddogs.com)

- Sound Effects Library.com (www.sound-effects-library.com)

Production Music Libraries:

- Digital Juice (www.digitaljuice.com)

- Fresh Music (www.freshmusic.com)

- Music Bakery (www.musicbakery.com)

- VideoHelper (www.videohelper.com)

Keep complex projects organized by grouping sound families on adjacent tracks. Don't place dissimilar elements such as dialog and sound effects on the same track.

Don't infringe on copyrights; license all sound effects and music for your productions.

Voice Rules!

The dialog track is the most important part to virtually every visual presentation. I use the word *dialog* as an umbrella term for all voice-based tracks including interviews, voice-over, reporter stand-ups, and, of course, dialog. Focus on capturing top-quality voice in the field, because most other sounds can be added in post-production.

With few exceptions, anchor all your dialog to the center channel. Place a little in the phantom center between the stereo L/R, too.

Occasionally, an off-screen voice can be interesting when placed in the surrounds, for example, when a character enters a room.

Always capture room tone and presence at *every* location. Room tone and presence smoothes and hides edits, making the finished track sound better.

Adding a 2db to 4dB EQ bump centered at 1.75kHz can help speech intelligibility.

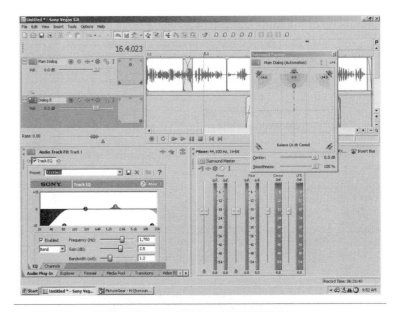

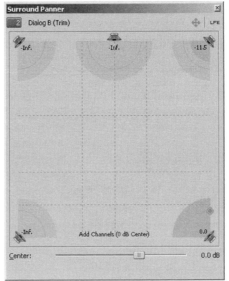

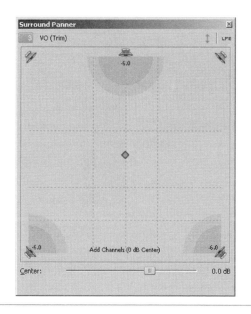

VOs can sound good right in the audience's face. Balance the center channel with the Ls/Rs as mentioned in the previous chapter.

Use the dialnorm setting as your dialog reference level. For example, make –27dB the average level of the dialog in your mix. All other elements in the mix should be subservient to that level. This ensures that the audience will understand the dialog and that no other sounds will overpower it. That doesn't mean that sounds can't be louder. They can, just not when dialog is present.

Both *Monsters Inc.* and *Finding Nemo* are two textbook examples of creative uses of surround sound mixing. *Monsters Inc.* even lets you turn off both the dialog and music and listen to just the sound effects tracks in 5.1. Understand that in an animated movie, every sound element must be created from scratch, so these DVDs are worth your critical study.

Statistics - Competition.wav	Left channel:	Right channel:
Cursor	00:00:00.000 (0)	00:00:00.000 (0)
Sample value	0 (-Inf. dB, 0.00 %)	0 (-Inf. dB, 0.00 %)
Minimum sample po	00:00:15.352 (677,054)	00:00:15.352 (677,054)
Minimum sample value:	,874 (-9.58 dB, -33.18 %)	-10,874 (-9.58 dB, -33.18 %)
Maximum sample position:	00:00:15.351 (676,982)	00:00:15.351 (676,982)
Maximum sample value:	8 (-5.82 dB, 51.14 %)	16,758 (-5.82 dB, 51.14 %)
RMS power:	-27.02 dB (4.45 %)	-27.02 dB (4.45 %)
Average value (DC Offset):	0 (-Inf. dB, -0.00 %)	0 (-Inf. dB, -0.00 %)
Zero crossings:	1,688.96 Hz	1,688.96 Hz

Depending on what you want to convey, group walla can work in stereo, the surrounds, or both. Leaving them out of the center creates a nice hole for the main dialog while still enhancing the scene.

Many of the ideas discussed in the music surround mixing chapter apply to audio post projects, too.

Sound Effects and Foley

Position hard sound effects with their on-screen visual counterparts. For instance, if a door closes screen left, the sound should emanate from that location. Foley sounds also benefit from matching the action for which they were created.

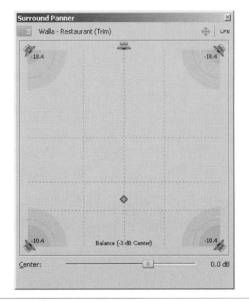

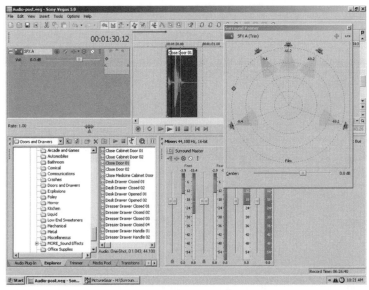

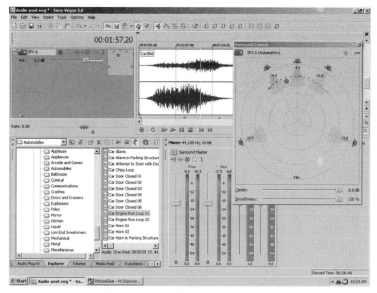

Dynamically pan sound effects as needed. If a car travels from right to left, the car sound effect should track the same way. You can do this with a mono sound panned to match the action. If you have a stereo effect, you may be able to leave it in place in the stereo L/R.

Adding reverb and other effects to a front sound effect and placing the affected sound only in the Ls/Rs can make a sound effect bigger.

A few well-placed uses of surround always stick out in listener's minds more than a constant bombardment of audio trickery.

Stacking similar sounds on top of each other can create richer and more complex sounds.

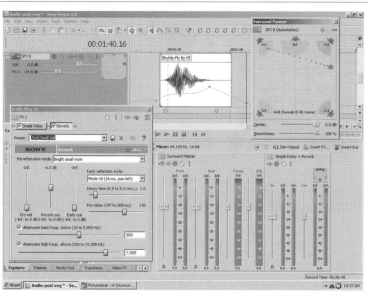

Here's my explosion recipe. Stack multiple recordings of explosions to create one unique sound. Start this in the front to match the action, then dynamically pan it over the audience to the rears. Use some reverb on the explosion (with a long pre-delay) routed to the rear, and bring that in to sustain the sound. Add debris sounds that fly out to the left right stereo, then back to the rear. Also, fly pieces from front center to rear center to make it fly over the audience (this works better with Dolby EX, though.) Also, add some extra thump routed to the LFE for more boom. Make that low-frequency rumble the last part to die away.

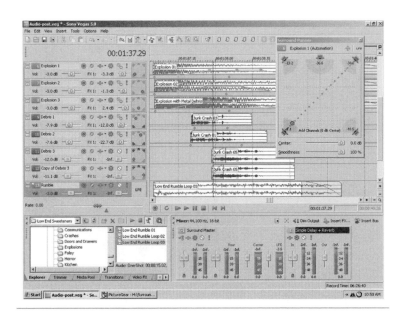

Backgrounds

Part of creating realistic and believable soundtracks is paying careful attention to the environments. Every place has a sound that is indicative of its function; a factory sounds different from a suburban park. While some environmental sounds, known as backgrounds, may come from your field recordings (specifically room tone and presence), the rest you may construct in post-production.

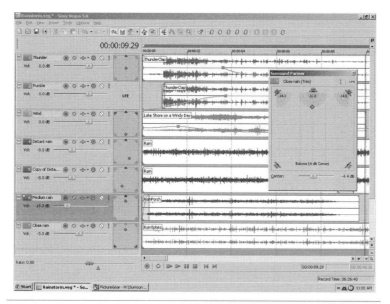

Layering is the secret to good backgrounds. Think close, middle, and distant sounds, and construct an environment with depth. To illustrate this point, think of a rainstorm. In the distance would be thunder; the swish of rain occupies the middle; and close-up features rain striking an object such as a sidewalk. Add other elements to sweeten the background as needed.

Immerse your audience in the environment.

Both stereo and mono backgrounds work well with surround. Mono sounds can be routed to speakers with corresponding reverb sent to opposites. Stereo sources can be routed to pairs.

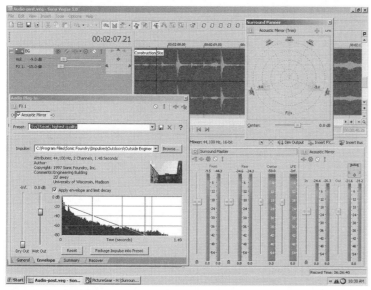

Create larger-than-life backgrounds by adding a mono or stereo background recording into the software. Duplicate the track. Assign the original to one position in the surround field.

Sounds that occur before a visual or continue from a previous scene often work well starting or finishing in the surrounds respectively.

Assign the duplicate to the opposite position. Cut the duplicate sound in half and reposition it so it starts at a different place than its counterpart. The two tracks are completely decorrelated, creating a better, more elaborate background than before.

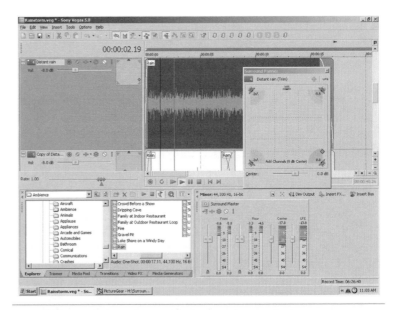

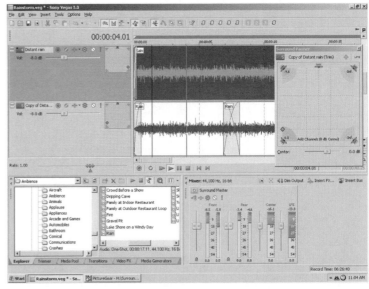

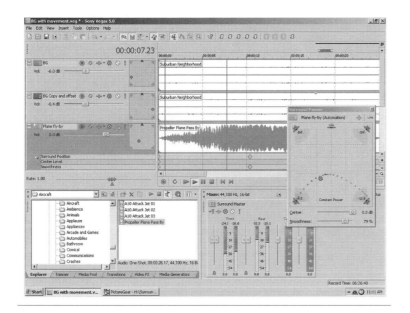

If your background is mostly static and assigned to a fixed area in the surround sound field, consider adding an occasional dynamically panned sound element. To a static neighborhood recording, add a plane flying in the surrounds only for a subtle effect.

Walter Murch and George Lucas world-ized much of the music in American Graffiti.

World-izing

Though your surround mixing software may have a variety of creative effects, sometimes the only way to get a particular effect to sound right is to record it in a place that matches the on-screen location. That isn't always possible, though. However, it may be possible to re-record the sound in a similar location, known as "world-izing. The technique involves playing sound effects, music, and sometimes dialog in a real location, recording the result, and then using the "world-ized" sound in the finished mix. Recording in true surround opens up more creative possibilities.

Sony's Acoustic Mirror plug-in, which ships with Sound Forge, is another way to add realistic ambiences to your tracks. The program uses specially prepared files that essentially capture only the characteristics of a space. These characteristics can then be applied to files making them sound as if they were recorded in that space.

Music

Source music should correspond to its on-screen origin. If the music comes from a radio, place it to match the radio's position. You may need to alter this somewhat as the scene changes. Use finesse so you don't distract the audience.

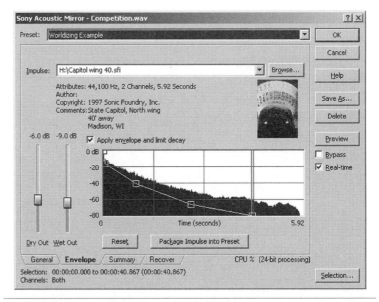

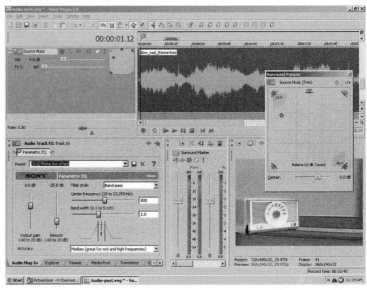

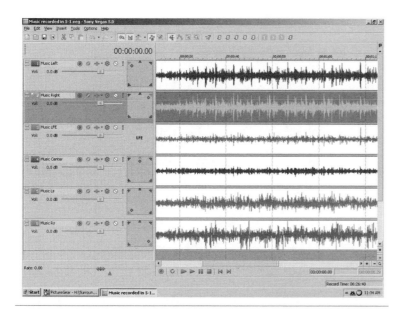

Placing underscore depends on many factors. If the music was recorded in true surround, placing the six tracks as designated makes sense.

Chances are the music recording is stereo only. Obviously, placing it in the front L/R stereo recreates the original recording. For a nice balance, keep dialog in the center speaker and the music in stereo.

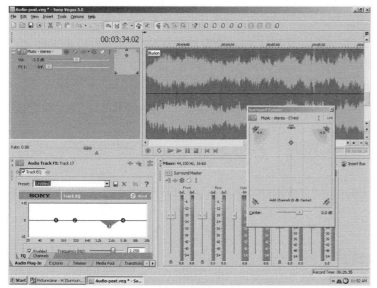

Pulling the music back into the room envelopes the audience more.

Adding reverb to play only in the surrounds, leaving the music in front L/R makes the music sound big and bold. Reversing that creates a unique effect, too.

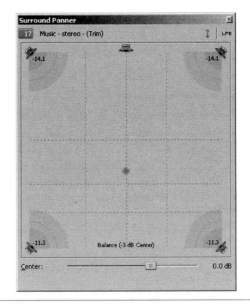

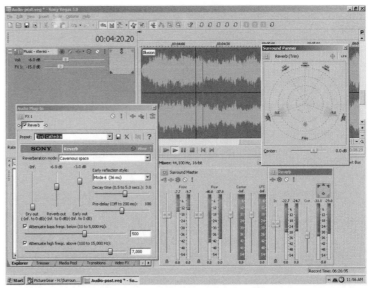

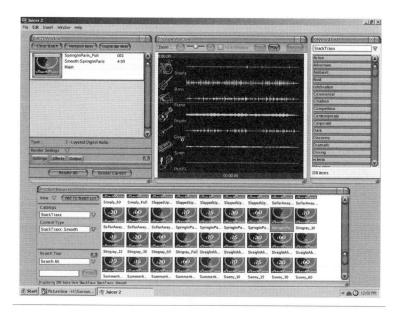

Digital Juice's StackTraxx music library (www.digitaljuice.com) includes multi-track layers of each song. With up to seven individual layers per tune, there are a myriad of surround sound mixing options available.

DM&E

Keeping the main three elements, Dialog, Music, and Effects, separate facilitates alternate-language soundtracks. These three parts are called stems and consist of three separate surround mixes (18 total tracks). The music and effects surround mix stems join the new language dialog track in a remix session. This approach maintains the original balance of the mix while offering some leeway to the alternate-language mixers to improve speech understanding.

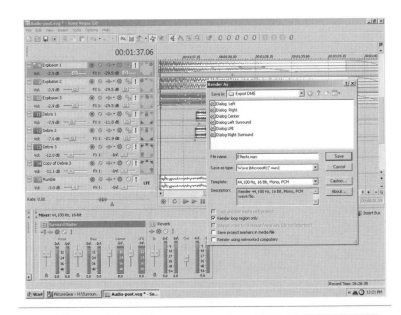

Final Sweetening

After balancing the elements that comprise the soundtrack, consider applying some gentle compression to even out the levels. The Sony Wave Hammer plug-in comes in a 5.1 configuration that is ideal for this purpose.

The same tool allows maximizing the volume to levels you indicate.

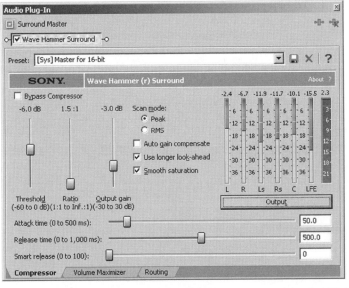

Audio Post Mixing

Working your way through an audio post project can be a demanding yet fascinating experience. With all the different sound elements to balance, there is much work to be done. As with the previous music chapter, it should be helpful to work through a project.

Dialog rules! Your audience must understand what people say!

Audio post-production begins after the picture edit is complete. Focus on the voice tracks first and make them sound their best. Dialog dominates nearly every visual project. Whether there are actors, interviews, or voice-over narrations (VO), it is crucial that your audience understand what people are saying.

Studio recordings along with audio recorded under controlled conditions usually require very little extra work to sound good. It's the field recordings that demand the extra care. Always work hard to record good, clean audio on location as it saves many headaches in post.

Don't forget about room tone and presence. Make sure you always record the "sound" of every location where you record voice. You can use this "noise" to help mask edits. How does this work? Our ear-brain combination is quite adept at listening to what's important and ignoring the background noise. Unfortunately, when background sounds come and go, such as during sound edits, we are distracted by them. If the noise is constant, however, we tend to tune it out.

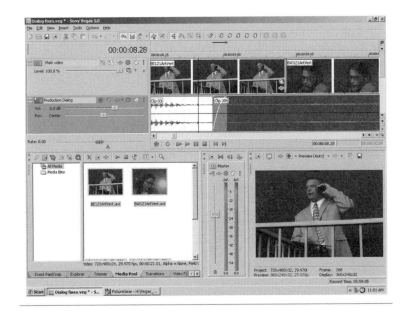

Most picture editors make the common mistake of cutting the dialog in the same place as the picture edit. This is rarely the best place to make a sound edit, because the shifting visual accentuates any sound change. Instead, cut the audio just before or after the picture cut or use crossfades or both.

The J cut edits the dialog when a person finishes speaking and before the visual edit.

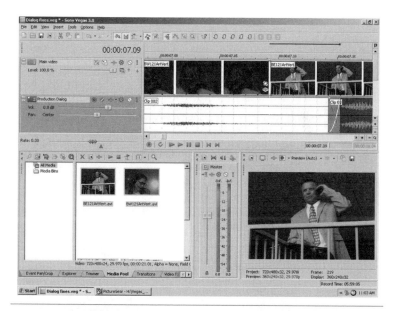

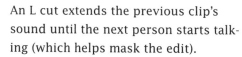

An L cut extends the previous clip's sound until the next person starts talking (which helps mask the edit).

Crossfading the audio makes smoothing these edits even easier.

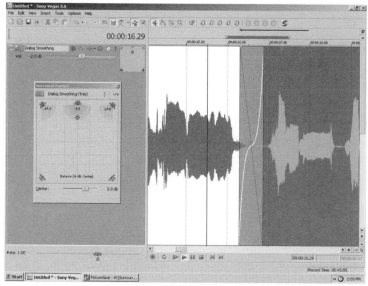

If your dialog tracks are noisy, you may need to resort to some sophisticated tricks to make them better for your audience. I heartily recommend the Sony Noise Reduction 2.0 plug-in, which works with any audio program that supports Direct-X plug-ins, such as Sony Sound Forge 7. Details about using these and other audio-restoration tools can be found in another book from this series: *Instant Sound Forge*.

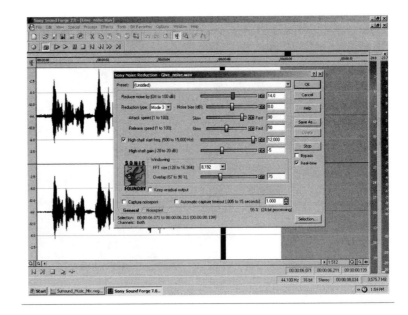

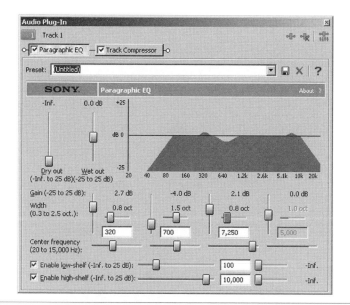

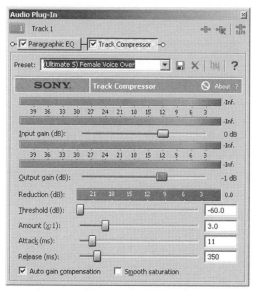

EQ and compression can make the dialog tracks shine. Try these settings:

- 100Hz low-shelf and 10,000Hz high-shelf

- 1db to 3dB bump at 160Hz for male or 320Hz for females for warmth

- Mid-range dip 2db to 4dB between 500–800Hz to minimize mud

- A little sparkle, 1db to 3dB, in the 7,000–8,000Hz area (listen for sibilance though)

- Gentle compression (post-EQ). Try 3:1 compression starting at –15dB

You already know that the center channel anchors your dialog to the screen, so placing the dialog is fairly straightforward. Leave a little in the front L/R, too.

If you have multiple tracks of dialog, consider inserting a mixer bus and have this one fader control the level of all dialog. Route each dialog track to this bus. Balance as needed.

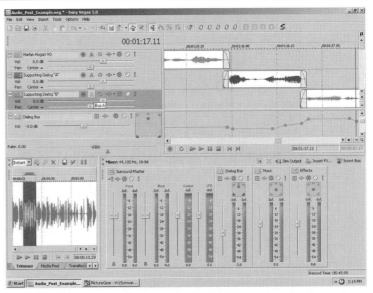

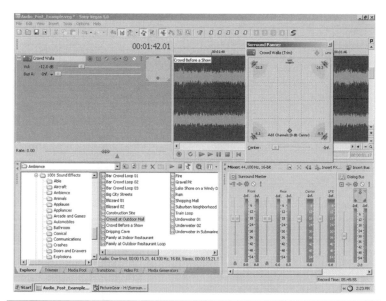

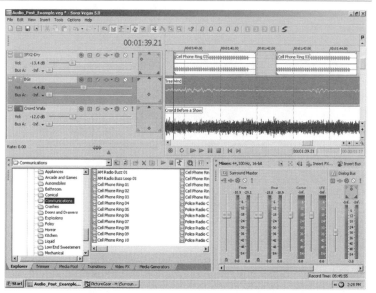

Placing dialog to one side, in the surrounds, or both works for a brief off-camera, off-screen voice. You can get more creative when placing crowd noises, called walla, as you can effectively put your audience in the middle of a crowd.

Turn your attention to sound effects. Many sounds available from libraries are often recorded dry and in-your-face. Therefore, they don't often sit well in a mix without some extra tweaking. The on-screen environment from which these effects originate helps complete the illusion. In other words, the background, environmental sounds help make the more up-front sound effects work right for the scene. Because of this, concentrate on the backgrounds before the hard effects.

Good backgrounds must work well with the dialog, augmenting or supplanting the room tone and presence used to smooth dialog edits. A well-recorded and well-placed background can work with dialog to create a very convincing soundtrack. Hard effects and music serve only to sweeten an already solid presentation.

The easiest and cheapest way to make your visual projects look better is to improve their sound!

Be aware of too many sounds building up in the center channel. Surround solves this issue by giving you alternative placement opportunities for your environmental, background sounds. Keeping backgrounds out of the center and using the front L/R and surround L/R speakers instead leaves a nice hole for the dialog to sit. Backgrounds recorded in true stereo (or true surround for that matter) make for a nice experience for the audience.

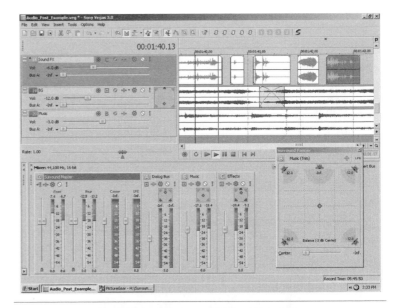

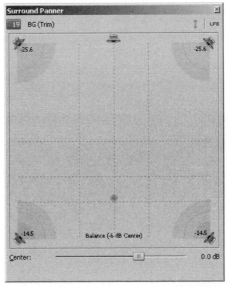

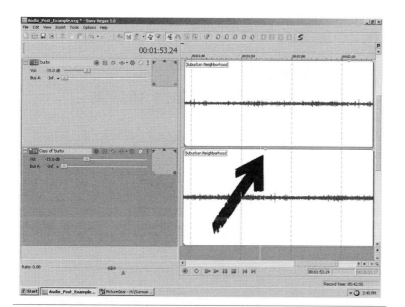

In the absence of true stereo, try this trick. Duplicate a background track. Offset the copy by about half its total length. Hard-pan the two tracks to opposite positions, either front L/R or rear L/R. This creates a pleasing pseudo-stereo effect and a more open background.

Don't forget about layers, too. Think foreground, middle ground, and farther away sounds and build a more realistic overall environment. Use the frequency spectrum, too, with solid lows, crisp highs, and in between.

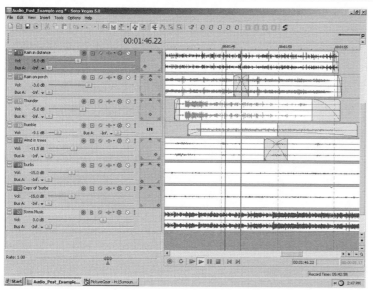

Use care to keep sounds that interfere with the voice out of the background mix, though. Dipping the EQ between 1,750–3,500Hz on background tracks can open up frequency room for consonants, which is what makes our speech more intelligible.

After backgrounds, turn to hard effects and use EQ, volume, and surround placement to fit these elements into the environment. Dynamic panning can work for certain sounds, such as a helicopter fly-over or for certain car-bys.

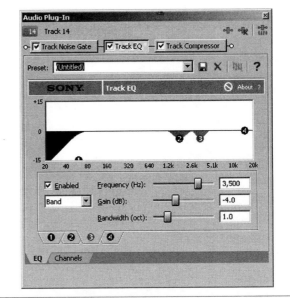

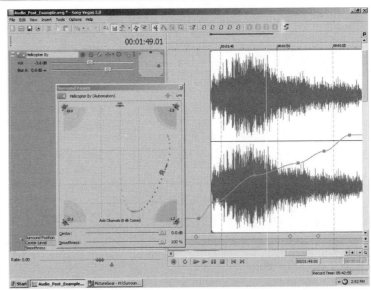

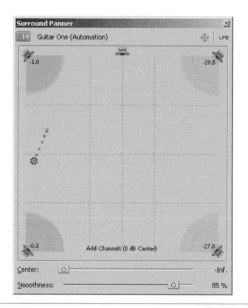

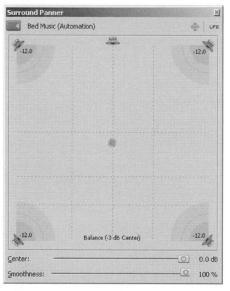

Using delays, reverb, or both in the surrounds can make foreground sound effects appear larger than life. The delay or reverb tail seems to sail right over the audience putting them in the sound itself. This is a terrific effect for horror-film-like "jumps"—sudden sounds that make the audience jump in their seats.

With a well-built soundtrack, music becomes another layer—the emotional icing on the cake, so to speak. With stereo music tracks, surround sound positioning can give them more depth.

Alternately, add a large reverb that plays solely in the surrounds. Route some of the music to this reverb, keeping the original music in conventional stereo. The music now envelopes the audience nicely.

With only a stereo music track, the surround options are somewhat limited. Granted, you can enhance the ambience of the music, but you can't truly affect the original balance or feature individual elements easily. If you had access to the original components that comprise the completed musical piece, you'd have more options.

For example, surround-izing the layers, or stacks, from Digital Juice's StackTraxx music library offers many creative alternatives. Instead of just a stereo music track, StackTraxx offers up to seven individual elements (for example, drums, guitar, bass, keyboards, and more) as separate tracks.

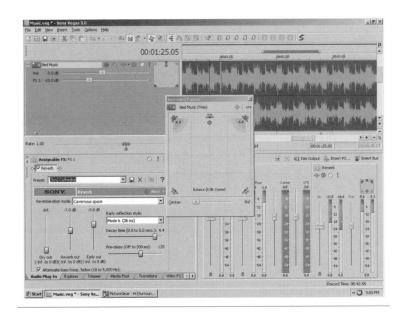

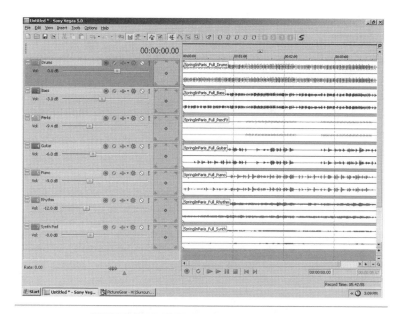

After using their Juicer 2 to export the individual layers to an empty folder, add them to individual tracks in your authoring application. Here "Spring In Paris" has seven stacks, one per track. After balancing the basic volume of the layers, turn to surround positioning.

Position the drums in the front stereo L/R. Turn the center channel and the surrounds off. This configuration maintains the original stereo balance of the drum part.

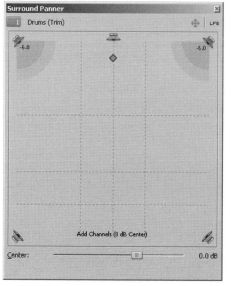

The bass part layer comes as a stereo file. Select just the left channel of the bass part and position it similarly to the drums: front stereo L/R and with its center and surrounds off, too. Make a copy of the bass track. This time, choose only the right channel. Add aggressive EQ to remove all the frequencies above 120Hz. Assign this to the LFE to add some extra low-end thump to the music track.

This track features an interesting percussion track. To emphasize it a little more, and to avoid masking the main drum part, turn off the stereo L/R speakers and instead balance the part midway between the center speaker and surround L/R. Balance the levels to place this track right in your listener's face.

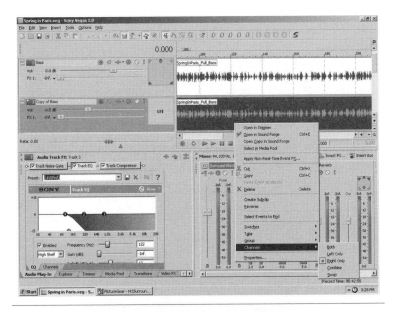

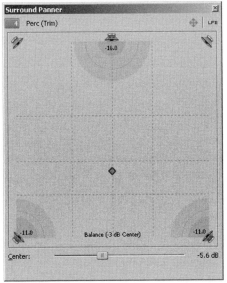

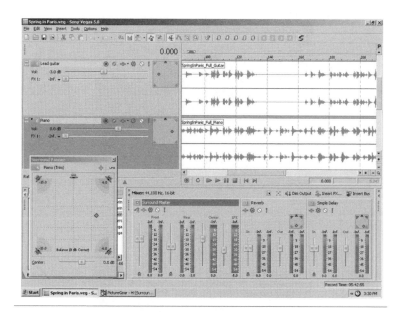

The lead guitar part and piano alternate as foreground tracks. Position the guitar about halfway between the front and rear speakers with about 70 to 80 percent primarily to the left. Turn the center off. Place the piano in the complementary space: halfway between front and rear and 70 to 80 percent to the right.

Place the rhythm guitar track dead center using the front and rear L/R, but turn the center channel off. This supplements the percussion track well once you balance their respective volume levels.

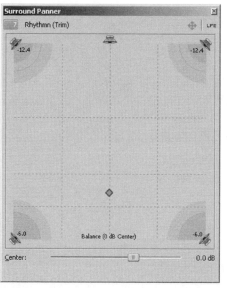

The synth pad part is just a sweetener, so direct it only to the L/R surrounds.

Next, add an insert FX with reverb. Choose a reverb setting with a long pre-delay. This is the amount of time between the original dry sound and the start of the reverb tail. Long pre-delays usually indicate larger rooms. Use the surround panner to position the reverb output to the rear L/R surrounds only. Also, make the reverb 100 percent wet (no dry sound). Balance the wet-dry mix using the FX sends available on your tracks or channels.

Send some of the drum part to this reverb. Adjust to taste. This effectively makes the drums sound bigger because their reverb tail plays behind the audience. The pre-delay keeps everything from getting muddy and also adds some movement to the drums, which appear to gently fly over the audience. Adjust for subtlety here, as you don't want people turning around as they listen.

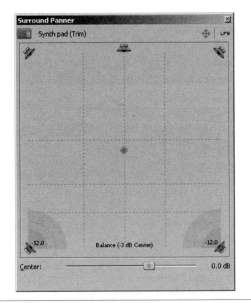

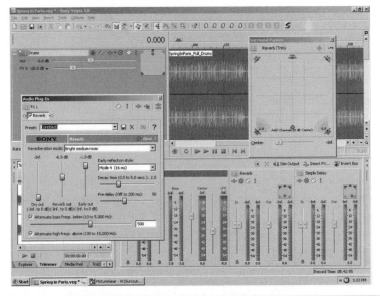

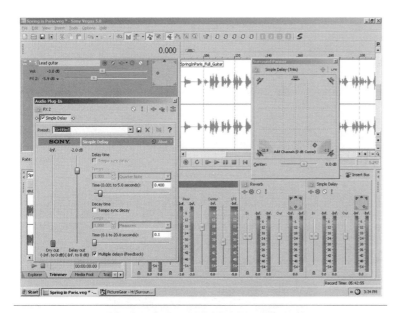

Add another Insert FX this time using a short delay. Assign this output to the R surround only. Send a little of the lead guitar part to this delay to make it cut through the mix a little better.

Finally, consider adding some dynamic panning to the parts, especially the piano and lead guitar. Don't go overboard. Feature the part when it makes musical sense by moving them more toward the front and center.

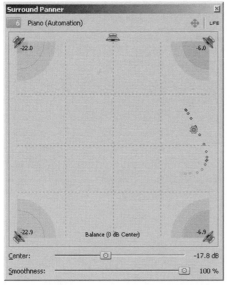

Making 5.1 Music with ACID

Sony's ACID Pro is another way to compose and deliver original music for your video productions. ACID uses pre-recorded loops of musical parts that you arrange on a timeline to craft music scores. Loops are simply snippets of performances that play seamlessly. What makes this work is that ACID automatically adjusts the musical key and tempo of loops to a single project tempo and key regardless of the loop's original settings.

To use the program, you preview loops, pick the ones you want, paint them in the Timeline, and play. The software ships with hundreds of loops to get you started, and there is massive support for additional loops from a variety of sources. Most importantly, loops come in many musical genres from orchestral to rock and virtually everything in between. Check out *Instant ACID* for more information on using this amazing software.

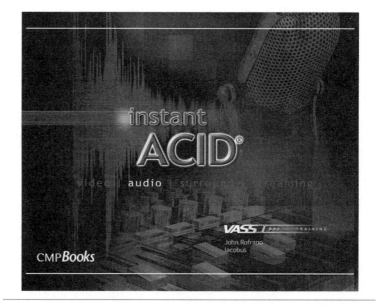

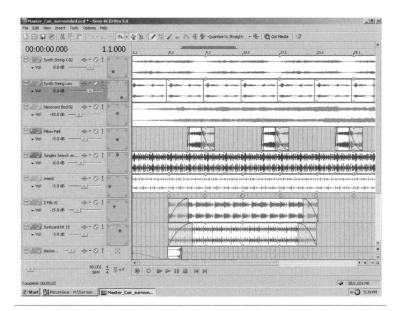

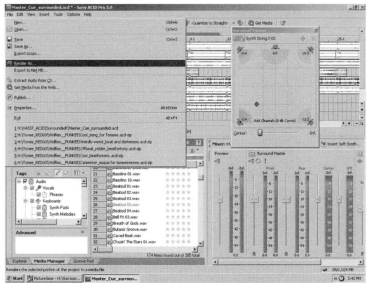

Best of all, ACID Pro 5 supports mixing in 5.1 surround. Once you've put your composition together, you can use its surround panners to place and balance your musical parts. Refer to Chapter 6 for ideas on bringing out the best surround mix for your project.

ACID Pro also makes it easy to import your surround music mix back to your video NLE, too. To export the individual buses that comprise your mix, choose File>Render As.

Select the Wave (Microsoft) (*.wav) format from the "Save as type" menu list. Choose the 44,100Hz, 16-bit, Mono, PCM template from the Template list. Notice the checkbox "Save each channel as a separate file" is selected (but grayed out). This exports the six channels of your surround mix into six separate mono files.

Name the file and choose a save location. ACID Pro uses this root name when rendering and exporting the individual channels. The software appends the appropriate surround channel name to this root name. Click OK.

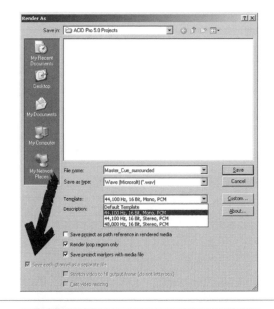

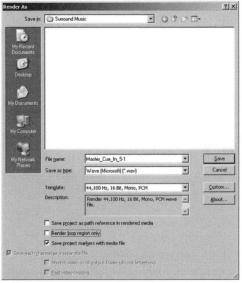

There are now six channels, appropriately named, carrying your surround mix.

Switch to your video NLE and add these six tracks to separate channels. Use each track's surround panner to position each track and recreate the ACID Pro music mix in your NLE.

Alternately, you could export each individual ACID Pro track, import them to the NLE, and then use its surround tools to mix the music instead. The choice depends on your tastes and the complexity of the project.

Chapter 8

Export and Encode Options

Once you've finished your surround sound mix, turn your attention to delivering your sonic master-piece to the world. This chapter examines exporting the files for encoding with separate, standalone software and encode options that may be built in to your authoring software.

Export to Multiple Files

Encoding software usually accepts the individual six channels that comprise your surround sound mix. In this situation, you need to export each channel as a standalone monaural file. Your encoder will indicate the desired format, usually either .wav or .aiff.

Also, check your encoder's instructions for details about handling the LFE. Specifically, look for whether to apply the low-pass filter or not and for specific cutoff frequency and roll-off settings.

The usual workflow is to export the individual buses of the surround mix, rendering them to the appropriate file format and saving them in a folder. You may need to name each file using specific conventions, or the software may do this automatically.

In Sony Vegas, for example, choose File>Render As to display the dialog box. Select a storage location for the final render, name the file, choose the .wav file format, and change the Template to either 48,000Hz or 44,100Hz, 16-bit, Mono, PCM.

Vegas saves all six files using the base name with the specific channel name appended to it.

Switch to your encoder of choice, import the six channels, and create the final encode suitable for DVD, DVD-A, SACD, and even web delivery.

DM&E Considerations

Exporting a DM&E 5.1 mix to its separate stems requires three separate renders. For example, to render the dialog stem, mute all music and effects tracks and buses. Render the six channels of the dialog using "Project-Name Dialog" as the base file name. Mute the dialog tracks and buses, unmute the music, and render the music as "Project-Name Music." Do the same for the effects (muting dialog and music for the render). When finished there will be 18 separate mono files ready for the next step. For example, an alternate-language dialog track could be recorded and join the M&E tracks for a new mix suitable for international delivery. Keeping the stems gives the mixer control over the final balance of the new dialog against the music and effects.

Dolby Digital AC-3 Metadata

Whether you are using a standalone encoder or an encoder that is built in to your surround authoring software, you need to understand the Dolby AC-3 options. The metadata that can be included with the AC-3 data stream is what ensures that your encode sounds its best.

The Dolby AC-3 format supports both stereo and 5.1 mixes. When choosing the stereo-only option, there are fewer settings available because most of the metadata settings relate to downmix options. There are some settings that apply, though. Set these accordingly. The remaining metadata settings are used by the decoder when it converts a surround mix to stereo.

I've already recommended that you create your own stereo mix from your original source material. This way you are not at the mercy of the decoder for your stereo downmix. That said, because you can't always control what a listener or viewer does, you should use the AC-3 metadata settings to craft the best encode, and the most faithful downmix, of your 5.1 surround mix.

AC-3 Audio Service Configuration

There are several settings that affect the quality and loudness of the final encode.

Bitstream mode—indicates the primary function of the encode. Choose from available options.

Audio coding mode—selects the encode format. The 3/2 designation is the 5 of the standard 5.1 surround sound option.

Enable LFE—the LFE can be turned on or off with this setting.

Sample rate—sets the sample rate for the encode. There are only three choices: 32kHz, 44.1kHz, and 48kHz. Generally, the higher the setting, the better the encode. However, higher settings generate larger file sizes, too.

Data rate—indicates the average data rate of the encoded file. Lower rates will reduce quality significantly but can save space. The minimum for 5.1 should be 384kbps, but 448kbps is a better choice. Higher rates can improve quality, but there is risk. For example, a DVD player may not be able to keep up with the data stream, and glitching may result.

Dialog normalization—sets the average level for dialog. This setting is so important that it's discussed in greater detail below. This is sometimes abbreviated dialnorm, too.

Bitstream Information

The most significant part of these settings have to do with downmix information.

Center mix level—sets the level reduction the decoder should apply when downmixing to stereo. The standard is –3dB. During the downmix, the center channel gets added to both the L/R front. Reducing the volume recreates the original balance.

Surround mix level—sets the level for the surround channels when added to the L/R front during a stereo downmix. Again, –3dB is standard, but you may prefer higher settings depending on what sound information your surround channels are carrying. You can even select none, if the balance is acceptable.

Set copyright bit—select this to add copyright protection and discourage unauthorized copying.

Mark as original bitstream—check this only if this is the original encode.

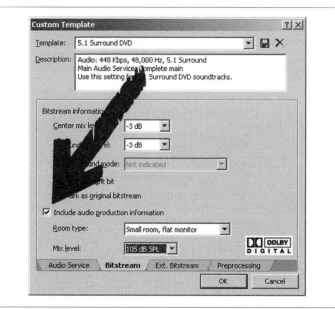

Include audio production information—these optional fields let you include information about the room type, speakers used, and mixing level. Note that the mix level uses the monitoring volume in SPL and the reference level used. For example, if the monitor calibration was −20dBFS pink noise to set 85dB SPL, the value is: 85dB + 20 = 105dB SPL.

Extended Bitstream

This optional metadata can be included in the AC-3 encode. This information allows fine-tuning of the downmix options.

Dolby Surround EX mode—indicates whether your mix is EX or not. Dolby Surround EX adds a non-discrete center surround channel; it is matrixed with the Ls/Rs channels.

A/D converter types—chooses the analog-to-digital converter used. Standard is fine.

Stereo downmix preference—directs the way an encoder handles the downmix.

- Lo/Ro—Adds the center channel to the front L/R and the surrounds to their respective front channels.

- Lt/Rt—Adds the center channel to the front L/R. Sums the surround channels to mono, adds them to both front L/R channels, the right 90 degrees out of phase.

- Lo/Ro and Lt/Rt center/surround mix level—adjusts the playback volume of these channels in their respective downmix scenarios.

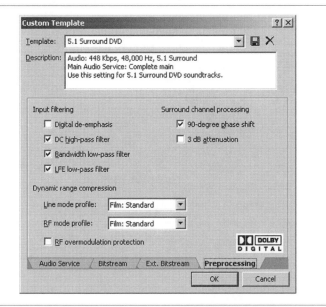

Preprocessing

Digital de-emphasis—applies a filter when an emphasis filter was used on the audio before the encode.

DC high-pass filter—removes any DC offset that may be present in the audio files. The digitizing process sometimes adds direct current (DC) to the recordings. This can misalign or offset the zero crossing (where a sound wave crosses the center line).

Bandwidth low-pass filter—prevents frequencies above the chosen Audio Bandwidth from reaching the encoder. This is essentially an anti-aliasing filter.

LFE low-pass filter—enables the LFE filter to keep frequencies above the cutoff point out of the LFE channel.

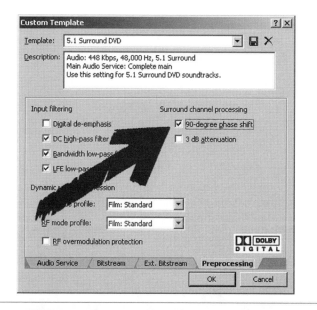

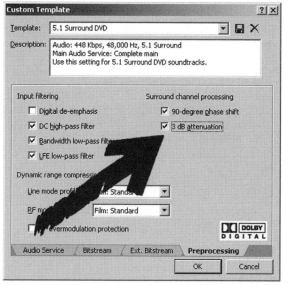

90-degree phase shift—applies the 90-degree phase shift to the right channel that is used by the decoder when downmixing from a 5.1 mix to a stereo Lt/Rt downmix.

3dB attenuation—reduces the level of the surrounds before encoding. This is not a downmix option. This setting compensates for film surrounds that are often 3dB louder. Television mixes often employ this level drop because viewers often sit closer to the surrounds than they should.

Dynamic range compression (DRC)—controls the difference between the loudest and the softest parts of the mix. It works in conjunction with the dialog normalization setting. This subject is discussed in detail below.

Line mode profile—sets the compression type used by the decoder for line level signals.

RF mode profile—indicates the compression type used by the decoder for antenna (RF) signals. RF overmodulation protection can also be applied.

Dialog Normalization

The dialog normalization or dialnorm setting indicates the dialog level based on the A-weighted average level over time. The AC-3 decoder uses the setting to adjust, or normalize, the audio output to a specific level.

The point of dialog normalization is to maintain consistent volume levels among different sources such as TV and DVD. Proper settings of the dialnorm parameters means a listener doesn't need to adjust the volume when changing TV channels or from TV to a DVD. The chosen listening level therefore stays constant for the listener. Even mixes without dialog, such as instrumental music, still need properly set parameters.

The dialog normalization settings range from −1 to −31dB in 1dB increments. The −31 setting indicates *no* level shift to the encoder. When the decoder sees an AC-3 stream with the −31 dialnorm setting, no level shift is applied to the material. The −31dBFS indicates the average A-weighted level of the dialog over time. That is 31dB below 0dB digital full-scale.

Using the –31 setting means your material will play at its pre-encoded level. However, there is another step called dynamic range compression (DRC) that can affect the volume of the mix.

Conversely, a –1 setting tells the decoder to apply the maximum level shift of 30dB. The formula is as follows:

- 31 + (dialnorm setting) = level shift
- 31 + (–27) = 4dB level shift

The point of the dialnorm is to maintain consistent volume levels and to feed the DRC profiles. This helps the listener have a more enjoyable experience.

You may be tempted to set a high dialnorm setting in an effort to raise the overall volume of your mix. Decoders have built-in overload protection to prevent high volume-level distortion. Unfortunately, this circuitry may adversely affect your mix by overly compressing it. Therefore, the two processes are counter-productive. You turn up the dialnorm setting and the decoder then turns the volume down because your mix is overloading the system.

General guidelines for dialog normalization

- Light jazz or New Age: –22
- Motion pictures: –27
- News or documentary: –15
- Pop: –27 to –30
- Rock 'n roll: –10 to –12
- Sports: –22
- Television shows: –18 to –20

Custom Template

Template: 5.1 Surround DVD

Description: Audio: 448 Kbps, 48,000 Hz, 5.1 Surround
Main Audio Service: Complete main
Use this setting for 5.1 Surround DVD soundtracks.

Input filtering
- ☐ Digital de-emphasis
- ☑ DC high-pass filter
- ☑ Bandwidth low-pass filter
- ☑ LFE low-pass filter

Surround channel processing
- ☑ 90-degree phase shift
- ☐ 3 dB attenuation

Dynamic range compression

Line mode profile: Film: Standard

RF mode profile: Film: Standard

☐ RF overmodulation protection

DOLBY DIGITAL

Audio Service / Bitstream / Ext. Bitstream / **Preprocessing**

OK   Cancel

Dynamic Range Compression

The Dolby AC-3 encoder allows specific settings to control the dynamic range of the material. Dynamic range is the difference between the loudest and the softest parts of the mix. There are times when a viewer or listener prefers the largest dynamic range, such as when watching a Hollywood blockbuster in a home theater. However, there are times when a reduced dynamic range is desired, such as late-night viewing.

Properly setting the dynamic range compression or DRC metadata tells the decoder to reduce the dynamic range of material based upon preset choices indicated when encoding. The listener can then decide whether to apply the DRC or not during playback. However, not all DVD decoders allow selecting the DRC. Stereo line level and RF set-top DVD players often rarely have selectable DRC options. Because these devices deliver only a stereo downmix, the DRC profile indicated by the metadata is nearly always applied.

DVD players with discrete outputs typically give the listeners the choice to activate the DRC or not. It may not be called DRC. It may be called "midnight mode" or something like that. For instance, one of my consumer surround systems calls it "night mode."

There are two modes of DRC. Line mode profile is used by two-channel set-top players and both stereo and 5.1 digital television. This compression profile can boost low-level and cut high-level signals. This effectively squeezes, or compresses, the dynamic range. The compression is scaleable, depending on the mode profile chosen and the dialnorm setting.

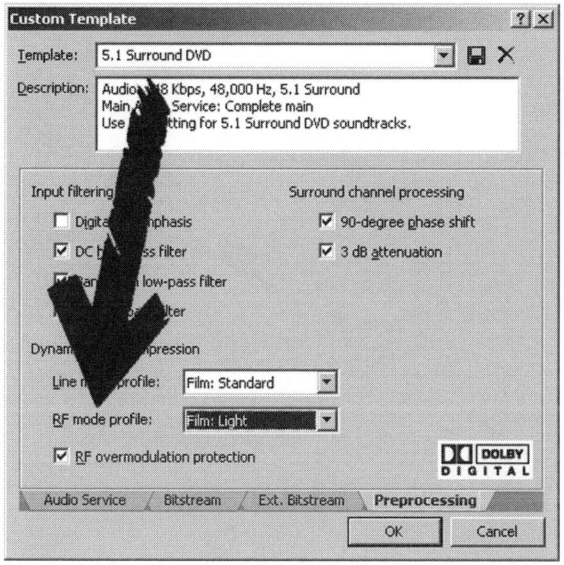

RF mode profile is used by set-top players that connect through an RF or antenna connection. There is no scaling of the compression. RF mode raises the overall level of the mix 11dB and limits the peaks to prevent overmodulation (distortion).

The DRC profiles determine how much low-level signals are boosted and high-level signals are cut. There are six profiles available from which to choose:

- Film Light
- Film Standard
- Music Light
- Music Standard
- Speech
- None

Though you can indicate a DRC profile, it applies *only* if the consumer chooses DRC mode during playback. Otherwise, only the dialnorm setting applies. However, many stereo-only devices automatically engage DRC when down-mixing.

Each DRC profile has different preset properties that cannot be adjusted.

- Max Boost—indicates the amount of low-level signal boost

- Boost Range—shows the range, in dB, of low-level signals boosted and the amount expressed as a ratio (see below).

- Null Band Width—this is the range where no compression is applied. This range is centered at the dialog normalization setting. The DRC profile then adjusts the other settings in relation to the dialnorm level setting. Improperly setting dialnorm defeats the whole purpose of the DRC metadata. If you set the dialnorm too high, the DRC overload protection circuity may adversely affect playback quality.

- Early Cut Range—sets the initial range where high levels are turned down or compressed and the amount expressed as a ratio (see below).

- Cut Range—shows the higher-level signals that are turned down, also expressed by a ratio (see below).

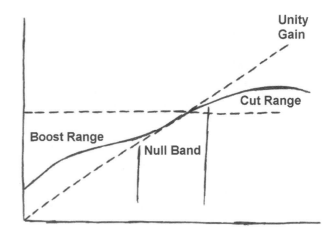

Film Light	Film Standard
• Max Boost: 6dB (below −53dB)	• Max Boost: 6dB (below −43dB)
• Boost Range: −53 to −41dB (2:1 ratio)	• Boost Range: −43 to −31dB (2:1 ratio)
• Null Band Width: 20dB (−41 to −21dB)	• Null Band Width: 5dB (−31 to −26dB)
• Early Cut Range: −26 to −11dB (2:1 ratio)	• Early Cut Range: −26 to 16dB (2:1 ratio)
• Cut Range: −11 to +4dB (20:1 ratio)	• Cut Range: −16 to +4dB (20:1 ratio)

Music Light	Music Standard
• Max Boost: 12 dB (below −65dB)	• Max Boost: 12dB (below −55dB)
• Boost Range: −65 to −41dB (2:1 ratio)	• Boost Range: −55 to −31dB (2:1 ratio)
• Null Band Width: 20dB (−41 to −21dB)	• Null Band Width: 5dB (−31 to −26dB)
• Early Cut Range: none	• Early Cut Range: −26 to −16dB (2:1 ratio)
• Cut Range: −21 to +9dB (2:1 ratio)	• Cut Range: −16 to +4dB (20:1 ratio)

The amount of compression is indicated as a ratio, such as 20:1. A 1:1 ratio means there is no compression; a 1dB signal level change results in a 1dB output (no or unity gain). At other ratios, the output is reduced by relative amounts. At 20:1, a 20dB increase in input level results in only a 1dB output level gain.

These are the preset settings for the DRC profiles.

Once again, the right settings are project-driven. Therefore, I suggest that you experiment with the modes and the dialnorm settings. Do some test encodes and evaluate them. Then, choose the best setting for your surround sound mix based on these tests.

Speech	None
• Max Boost: 15dB (below –50dB) • Boost Range: –50 to –31dB (5:1 ratio) • Null Band Width: 5dB (–31 to –26dB) • Early Cut Range: –26 to –16dB (2:1 ratio) • Cut Range: –16 to +4dB (20:1 ratio)	• The dialogue normalization still applies. If you set dialnorm to –31 dB in conjunction with this setting, your mix will play back at its original volume and dynamic range. You effectively defeat the DRC and the –31 dialnorm reflects no signal normalization or boost.

Custom Template   [?][x]

Template: DTS 48kHz 5-1 channel export   ▼ 💾 ✕

Description: Render 48,100 Hz, 16 Bit, Mono, PCM wave file for DTS

Format: PCM (uncompressed)   ▼

Attributes: 48,000 Hz, 16 Bit, Mono   ▼

Sample rate (Hz): 48,000   ▼

Bit depth: 16   ▼

Channels: Mono   ▼

                          OK   Cancel

DTS

DTS Coherent Acoustics Audio offers an additional or alternative format for delivering your surround mixes on DVD. There are both hardware- and software-based encoders available. Of utmost importance when using DTS is proper synchronization between the picture and the soundtrack. DTS embeds timecode to maintain sync. However, some DTS encoders rely only on the audio and video starting on the same frame. Check with your encoder for specifics.

DTS prefers your source audio tracks, prior to encoding, to have the 48kHz sample rate.

Settings available for DTS encodes include:

- Bitrate selection—choose either 754.5kbps or 1,509.25kbps. DTS recommends the higher rate unless space is at a premium in the disc.

- LFE—select whether to include or exclude the LFE from the final encode.

- Surround Channel Attenuation—applies a –3dB volume adjustment to the surrounds.

- Resolution—select the bit-depth from either 16, 20, or 24 bits.

DTS does not support metadata, so there are no settings for dialog normalization or DRC profiles as with Dolby Digital AC-3.

Custom Template

Template: 5 Mbps HD 720-24p Video, 5.1 Surround

Description: Audio: 128 Kbps, 48,000 Hz, 5.1 Surround.
Video: 23.976 fps, 1280x720, WMV V9 CBR Compression,
Smoothness 0.
Use this setting for high-quality HD video playback from a local hard

☑ Include audio

Mode: CBR

Format: Windows Media Audio 9 Professional

Attributes: 128 kbps, 44 kHz, 5.1 channel 16 bit (A/V) CBR

192 kbps, 96 kHz, 2 channel 24 bit (A/V) CBR
192 kbps, 96 kHz, 5.1 channel 24 bit (A/V) CBR
256 kbps, 44 kHz, 2 channel 24 bit (A/V) CBR
256 kbps, 44 kHz, 5.1 channel 16 bit (A/V) CBR
256 kbps, 44 kHz, 5.1 channel 24 bit (A/V) CBR
256 kbps, 48 kHz, 2 channel 24 bit (A/V) CBR
256 kbps, 48 kHz, 5.1 channel 16 bit (A/V) CBR
256 kbps, 48 kHz, 5.1 channel 24 bit (A/V) CBR
256 kbps, 88 kHz, 2 channel 24 bit (A/V) CBR
256 kbps, 96 kHz, 2 channel 24 bit (A/V) CBR
256 kbps, 96 kHz, 5.1 channel 24 bit (A/V) CBR
384 kbps, 44 kHz, 2 channel 24 bit (A/V) CBR
384 kbps, 44 kHz, 5.1 channel 16 bit (A/V) CBR
384 kbps, 44 kHz, 5.1 channel 24 bit (A/V) CBR
384 kbps, 48 kHz, 2 channel 24 bit (A/V) CBR
384 kbps, 48 kHz, 5.1 channel 16 bit (A/V) CBR
384 kbps, 48 kHz, 5.1 channel 24 bit (A/V) CBR
384 kbps, 88 kHz, 2 channel 24 bit (A/V) CBR
384 kbps, 96 kHz, 2 channel 24 bit (A/V) CBR
384 kbps, 96 kHz, 5.1 channel 24 bit (A/V) CBR

Project Au

Windows Media 9

To deliver 5.1 via the web (and on
CD-ROM), Windows Media 9 and above
offers support for surround sound.
You can select either constant bit rate
(CBR) or quality variable bit rate (VBR).
Choose the bitrate of the encoded file,
and indicate its bit depth (16- or 24-
bit). There are no other settings in the
encoder.

Testing the Encode

When using software encoders, it is not possible to audition the results during the encode itself. Few (if any) products play encoded files. Instead, you may need to author a DVD with your finished AC-3 or DTS encoded audio. Once completed, play back the disc and evaluate the mix and the encode.

Since DVDs support multiple soundtracks (up to eight), you could include several different mixes or encodes on one disc. With your DVD remote, switch back and forth between the tracks and decide what's best for the project. I highly recommend that you evaluate these tests on a variety of different systems, too. Take notes and use what you learn for the encode destined for the final disc.

Conclusion

Final Thoughts

This book provided the basic foundation on which to build your surround sound endeavors. Are you excited about the creative possibilities open to you with your own work?

I also know that no single book can tell you everything you need to know about a subject. Therefore, I encourage you to keep learning about audio production and surround sound techniques. Listen to what other professionals are saying about and doing with surround sound. Go to the movies, rent DVDs, buy music mixed specifically in 5.1. Keep expanding your knowledge and your own work will be so much better.

Also, to augment your education, I highly recommend the following additional resources.

Dolby (www.dolby.com) offers several free documents (in PDF format) that provide additional details:

- *A Guide to Dolby Metadata*
- *5.1 Production Guidelines*
- *5.1 Music Production Guidelines*

DTS (www.dtsonline.com) also has a useful document:

- *DVD-Video Production with DTS Coherent Acoustics Audio*

If you plan to author music in surround sound, get the Recording Academy's Producers and Engineering wing (www.grammy.com) guidelines:

- *Recommendations for Surround Sound Production*

Surround Professional Magazine (www.surround-pro.com) has up-to-date information along with an annual conference dedicated to surround sound.

I'm happy to help you further, too. Drop by Digital Media Net (www.dmnforums.com) and you'll find me co-hosting the Acid, Vegas, and Sound Forge forums.

Also, feel free to stop by my Web site at www.jeffreypfisher.com or e-mail me at jpf@jeffreypfisher.com

Surround sound is an evolving field. I hope you now feel empowered to experiment freely with your own work. I'll be listening!

Jeffrey P. Fisher

Glossary

Some of these audio terms are relevant to surround sound directly, and other terms are related to the audio and video industry in general. Some of the terms are "new" language adapted from the analog world.

AAF Advanced Authoring Format, a format that allows applications to share raw or rough cuts.

A/D converter Analog-to-digital converter. Many A/Ds are also D/As, which convert digital back to analog for monitoring.

AC-3 Dolby's audio compression scheme, third generation. Both stereo and 5.1 surround format files may be encoded to AC-3. Many software tools support the encoding of stereo audio and import of 5.1 AC-3 files.

ACM Audio Compression Manager, developed by Microsoft as the standard interface for signal processing of audio data in the Windows environment, particularly geared towards the WAV file format. Some tools allow custom ACM processes.

ADC Another name for analog-to-digital converter. See DAC.

ADR Automated dialog replacement, the process of replacing actors' lines, recorded on location, with clean and clear audio recorded in a studio environment. ADR was very popular in the '60s and '70s, and then was not quite as common through the '80s. The high volume of film technology today often calls for ADR. ADR is also often called "looping" but should not be confused with audio loops such as those from ACID.

AIFF Audio Interchange File Format. It can be used for storing audio in high- or low- resolution formats and sharing them between computer systems. It is predominantly an Apple format.

Aliasing The undesired shifting of frequencies, particularly problematic at low sampling rates, where there aren't enough samples to describe or recreate a sound. For instance, if you have a 24kHz tone and are sampling at a rate of 48kHz and the audio tone rises, in theory you won't be able to record frequencies higher than the 24kHz tone. What really happens is that the sample actually becomes a recreation of a lower tone, creating an obnoxious distortion of the original tone.

Amplitude The height of a waveform measured from the middle, where silence would be indicated. If no waveform is drawn, then the audio section is silent; the measurement from center to the highest point in the graphical drawing is the value of the amplitude. Acoustic amplitude is measured in dB (see decibels). The louder the signal, the higher the amplitude, regardless of the measurement format (peak, RMS, Instant, etc.).

Anchor point A bitstream location that serves as a random point. An example is an MPEG I-frame.

Anti-aliasing Oversampling, smoothing filters, interpolation of sound. It is the opposite of aliasing.

Artifact Distortion of a picture or a sound signal. With digital video, artifacts can result from overloading the input device with too much signal or from excessive or improper compression.

Aspect ratio Ratio of width to height in dimensions of an image. For example, the frame aspect ratio of NTSC video is 4:3, whereas widescreen frame sizes use the more elongated aspect ratio of 16:9 or 1.85.1

Asset Any digital file that is part of the library or project.

Audition Preview audio or video.

ATSC Advanced Television Systems Committee, which determines voluntary technical standards of acquisition, authoring, distribution, and reception of high-definition television.

AVI Audio-Video Interleaved, the format or scheme created by Microsoft for synchronizing and compressing analog audio and video signals. AVI is also the file format used by video for Windows.

Attenuate An analog term referring to the decreasing of the audio level. Usually described in decibels.

Audio file Audio stored in any digital format. This is not to be confused with audiophile, an audio affecionado.

B-frame In interframe compression schemes (e.g., MPEG), a highly compressed, bidirectional frame that records the change that occurred between the i-frames before and after it. B-frames enable MPEG-compressed video to be played in reverse. Contrast with I-frame and P-frame.

Balance The difference in level or apparent loudness between Right and Left in a stereo audio signal. See Panning.

Balanced cable A cable that contains two conductors carrying audio, plus a shield for the ground that carries no audio. Professional mic cables are always balanced.

Bandwidth The range of frequencies in an audio file, EQ, or other signal or device that passes a signal. This term also refers to the data rate of a streaming file.

Bass Low frequencies in the overall spectrum of sound. Bass is approximated in the 0Hz to 300Hz region of the frequency spectrum.

Bed Background music or sound effect laid under a voice-over. Typical term in television and radio.

Bitmap A graphic image comprised of individual pixels, each of which has a value that define its relative brightness and color.

Bit depth The number of bits in a sample. The greater the number of bits, the greater the resolution of the audio file, and therefore the more accurately the digital file will reproduce the original audio image.

Blumlein Technique A stereo microphone technique using two bidirectional (figure of 8) microphones crossed against each other.

Boost Raising the volume of an audio signal.

BPM Beats per minute and sometimes beats per measure. It's an indication of tempo.

Brick wall When digital audio hits the 0dB threshold, bits are truncated and lost. This is known as hitting the brick wall as there is no recovery from lost bits. It is a digital form of distortion.

Bright Descriptive term to describe high frequencies. If a sound is bright, then it contains a number of high frequencies. If the sound is not bright, then it may be considered dull, containing few high frequencies. Sibilance is typically fairly bright, allowing breath and Ss, Ps, Ts, Ps, and other sibilant sounds to be heard.

Bumper Stock audio identifying the television, radio, or cable station, or perhaps designating a corporate audio ident, such as the famous Intel sound.

Bus A feature used in hardware mixers and some software mixers to route audio from place to place, such as submixes, effects, and other processes.

Capturing Capturing source video for use on a computer. If analog, the captured video is converted to digital.

Channel Each component color that defines a computer graphic image—red, green, and blue. Colors are carried in separates channel so each may be adjusted independently. Channels may also be added to a computer graphic file to define masks.

Chapter A new segment of an existing work as the work is broken up into subject- or scene-specific sections.

Chorus (FX) A series of short, modulated delays with slight shifts in pitch to create the effect of multiple voices, stemming from one voice. This effect allows a solo instrument to have the sound of an ensemble due to the slight differences in timing and pitch.

Clip A digitized or captured portion of video.

Clipping Distortion, resulting from when audio is "clipped off" after exceeding maximum levels. Distortion can be caused at input, output, or processing stages. In the digital realm, clipping becomes brick-walling. Distortion can also mean the cropping of peaks (overmodulation) of the white or the black portions of a video signal.

Codec Contraction of compression/ decompression algorithm used to encode and decode data such as sound and video files. Common codecs include those that convert analog video signals to compressed digital video files (e.g., MPEG), or ones that convert analog sound signals into digital sound files such as Windows WMA file format. Surround audio is often encoded to the AC3 codec.

Compilation A music-industry term for a music playlist.

Compress (dynamic range) To reduce the amount of dynamic range of an audio signal, making the overall output more consistent. A compressor acts like an automated fader, bringing loud portions of an audio signal to a more quiet point, and raising the level of quiet sections to match louder transient peaks.

Compress (file size) Resampling, reducing a file size for streaming or sharing over the Internet or an intranet. Usually a lossy process, causing some loss of audio quality. Real Media, MPEG, MJPEG, Microsoft WMV and WMA are all examples of compressed media. Use Apple's Compressor to compress media.

Copyright Just as the word implies, the right to copy. Any composition is copyrighted as it's completed. No one has the right to copy the composition, video, or other art forms without the permission of the author of the work.

CTI Current Time Indicator.

Cue A specific piece of music composed to play at a specific moment in time. The moment the composition is to play is called a cue point. A list of cue points is called a cue list, generally determined in the spotting session (see Spotting). Spotting may also refer to a marker in some dialogs. Cue also refers to setting up a piece of media (audio or video) to play at a specific trigger, such as a DJ cueing up music or video to play at the press of a button.

Cut To delete a section from a digital event. Also refers to a composition, typically in album form, with the composition being a "cut" of an album. Also refers to reducing frequencies in an equalizer, as in "cutting the bass" from a mix, meaning to reduce the amount of bass in a mix.

Cutoff frequency The frequency at which audio is deeply attenuated or reduced. Low-pass and high-pass filters both center around a cutoff frequency. The higher the cutoff, the less original audio is allowed to be heard.

DARS Digital Audio Reference Signal.

DAW Digital Audio Workstation.

Decibel (dB) A measurement of sound describing electrical power referenced to 1 milliwatt. So 0dBm is equal to 1 milliwatt, or 1m. The abbreviation dB may refer to dBu, dBv, or dBm. To a listener, audio must be 6dB louder to appear to be twice as loud, while electronically, only 3dB of voltage difference are required for the same result. This is why a 200-watt amplifier is not twice as loud as a 100-watt amplifier.

Deinterlace The process of removing artifacts that result from the nature of two-fields-per-frame (interlaced) video.

Destructive/non-destructive Destructive editing alters the original file and cannot be undone. In the DAW and NLE worlds, destructive editing is often used to save disk space. With the cost of hard drives coming down, destructive editing is less prevalent than it was not long ago. Non-destructive editing does not affect the original file regardless of what processes are applied.

Digitize Converting analog to digital audio or video. The moment analog information is stored on a hard drive by whatever means it arrives there, it becomes digitized.

Distortion The point at which audio no longer maintains its original integrity, intentionally or not. Audio that exceeds physical or electronic limitations becomes distorted. Also used as an effect, particularly on guitars, violins, and other stringed instruments. See Clipping.

Dolby/Dolby Labs Founded in 1965, Dolby Laboratories is known for the technologies it has developed for improving audio sound recording and reproduction including their noise reduction systems (e.g., Dolby A, B, and C), Dolby Digital (AC-3).

Downconvert A term used to describe the format conversion from a higher-resolution input signal number to a lower display number, such as 1080i input to 480i display.

DTS Digital Theatre Surround. DTS is a competitor to AC3. It is slightly more robust with a higher data rate. It was developed in part by Steven Spielberg.

Dull Opposite of Bright. Sound that is dull lacks high frequencies. It may be perceived as unexciting.

DV/DV25 Digital video, the most common form of DV compression. DV25 uses a data rate of 25mbps per second or 3.6MB per second.

DVD Digital Versatile Disk, used for storing images, data, audio, and system backups. The standard for MPEG storage and display of moving images.

DVD Start Sony's nomenclature for the first-play video in a DVD project.

Dynamic range The difference between loud and quiet passages in an audio performance. Sometimes referred to in terms of how loud audio is permitted to go without distortion or how quiet audio may go before noise is heard.

Dynamics Varying levels of amplitude that audio demonstrates throughout the project.

EDL Edit decision list. The EDL is often used to move projects from one software application to another, containing time-pointer and other information relative to the project and how it is managed.

Effects (FX) Signal processors are referred to as effects or FX. Reverbs, choruses, delays, phasers, flangers, are all referred to as FX.

End action An instruction given to a playlist or video file, indicating what the DVD player should do following the end of a video's play. An end action might instruct the DVD to play the next video on the disc, return to a menu, or simply stop.

Envelope A graphic display of a volume, pan, or FX control, allowing automated control over the behavior of specific parameters in the mixing of sounds. Also referred to as the acoustical contour of a sound, its attack, decay, sustain, and release (ADSR).

Envelope point A handle or node inserted on an envelope used to control various parameters of volume, pan, and automated FX functions in a DAW or NLE application.

Equalizer (EQ) A plug-in that allows specific frequencies to be manipulated and controlled. Bass, mid-range, and treble frequencies are all broken down into specific bands and are controllable via sliders or dials, to cut or boost specific frequencies. This is one of the most important tools found in any DAW or NLE tool, as it allows specific contouring and shaping of audio events to help it fit more easily with other audio events.

Export Sending media from one application to another, such as exchanging audio from an NLE to a DAW. See Import.

FPS Abbreviation for frames per second; the standard for measuring the rate of video playback speed. A rate of 30fps is considered real-time speed, and a rate of 24fps is considered animation speed. At 12–15fps, the human eye can detect individual frames, causing video to appear jerky.

Fade A gradual decrease or increase of video or audio. Audio fades from audible to silent; video fades from visible to black. A fade may also be used to transition from one event to another (crossfade).

Field One complete vertical scan of a picture that has 262.5 lines (NTSC). A complete television frame comprises two fields; the lines of field 1 are vertically interlaced with those of field 2 for 525 lines of resolution according to the NTSC standard.

FireWire An IEEE1394 high-bandwidth, high-speed interface created by Apple as an industry standard for file I/O, not limited to, but commonly related to video and audio. Also used as a hard drive interface. Sony calls this i-Link.

Foley The art of creating ambient sound for film, synchronized with action on the screen. A Foley room used to record audio for film contains various surfaces and equipment to simulate or imitate sounds heard in the field-recorded audio for film or video.

Frame Film moves at 24 frames per second, meaning that 24 individual pictures or "frames" are required for each second of film or video. An extracted still image or where the playhead parks in an NLE is referred to as a frame. NTSC video moves at 29.97 frames per second, and PAL video moves at 25.00 frames per second.

Frequency In audio this refers to how fast a waveform or audio signal repeats itself. Measured in Hertz. Low frequencies are 20Hz to 250Hz; mid-range frequencies are 250Hz to 2kHz; and high frequencies are 2kHz to 20kHz.

Gain The amount that a sound is amplified from its original value; the change in its power point. See Amplitude.

GOP Group of Pictures.

Handles In a captured video file of a specific length, additional time before and after the specified length. Extra video is captured for editing purposes. The word "handles" is also used to describe envelope points in some DAW or NLE software.

HDTV High-Definition Television. HDTV is rapidly becoming a world standard in both 720p and 1080i formats.

HDV High Definition Video, not to be confused with HDCam or other formats. HDV is a 25Mbps video stream when recorded at 1080i resolution, and 19Mbps when recorded at 720p resolution.

Hz Hertz. KiloHertz is abbreviated kHz, and megahertz is abbreviated MHz.

I/O In/Out. Relating to video and audio, generally referring to hardware used to get audio in or out of a computer. See AD Converter.

I-frame In interframe compression schemes (e.g., MPEG), the key frame or reference video frame that acts as a point of comparison to P- and B-frames and is not rebuilt from another frame. An I-frame is the opposite of a B-frame and a P-frame.

Import To open a computer file with an application that did not create the file. Most NLEs can import files ending in .wav, .aiff, .wma, .wmv, jpg, .png, .mov, .m2v, and many other file formats.

Interframe compression A compression algorithm such as MPEG that reduces the amount of video information by storing only the differences between a frame and those before it.

Intraframe compression Compression that reduces the amount of video information in each frame on a frame-by-frame basis. Compare to Interframe compression.

IVTC Inverse Telecine. The process of converting 30fps media to 24fps media by removing pulldown.

KHz Kilohertz.

Latency The processing time between audio's origin or trigger point and when the signal is actually heard.

Latency above 10 milliseconds (ms) is unacceptable in a recording situation, as there is no way to properly match recorded audio with audio being recorded, resulting in out-of-time files. With Asio devices, most DAWs and NLEs are capable of extremely low-latency recording.

Layback Importing, matching, and dubbing a finished score or soundtrack back to the video master. Exporting audio from ACID or Soundtrack and importing to an NLE for final rendering can be considered a layback.

Layover Recording audio from an analog source to a multitrack, DAW, or audio portion of an NLE.

Layout The manner in which a workspace or surface is defined and viewed.

Letterbox A format for the display on television of video in the motion-picture aspect ratio. The aspect ratio of motion pictures is wider than those of standard televisions. To preserve the original aspect ratio of a motion picture, a motion picture includes black bars at the top and bottom of the screen when played on television.

Loop A segment or slice of audio that repeats without any indication of the end of the segment adjoining the beginning of the segment. Looped audio sequences are wonderful for seamless menu looping in DVD authoring tools.

M&E Music and Effects.

Master The finished product after a final mix has been created and the final mix components have been finalized with all EQ, compression, and volume settings. The final product on hard disk, tapes, or authored DVD is referred to as "the master."

Media Another term for a file, related to audio, video, graphic, etc. in the digital environment.

Mic Microphone.

Midrange Audio found in the frequency bandwidths of 250Hz to 2KHz.

Moire Visual distortion caused by the interference of similar frequencies, or the waving effect produced by the convergence of lines. See Aliasing.

Monitor Any device that allows audio or video to be seen or heard. Audio monitors are in the form of speakers or headphones; video monitors are in the form of a television, CRT, plasma, or LCD.

Mono A single channel of audio information as opposed to stereo audio containing two channels.

MP3 MPEG Audio Layer 3 compression format. Used to compress files for delivery over the Internet or for playback on portable hardware devices to save space and bandwidth.

MPEG Abbreviation for Motion Picture Experts Group, a group that defined a standard for compression of video or audio media.

MPEG-2 An extension of the MPEG-1 compression standard designed to meet the requirements of television broadcast studios. MPEG-2 is the broadcast quality video found on DVDs and requires a hardware decoder (e.g., a DVD-ROM player) for playback.

MTC MIDI time code. NLEs and DAWs often use MTC to act as a slave or master to other devices.

Multimedia Media and files that contain audio, video, graphics, MIDI, animation, or text in any combination. It is a broadly used term to describe

nearly any form of media.

Music compilation A series of audio assets that behave like a playlist in a DVD project.

Mute A software or hardware switch that prevents audio from being heard on a channel or channels.

Near-field monitors Small reference monitors or speakers within close proximity of the engineer or editor. They are used in small rooms or for monitoring at low-volume levels in larger rooms. They are generally less fatiguing to the ear.

NLE Non-linear editor.

Normalize A digital process for increasing the level of an entire audio file to a preset level without clipping.

NTSC National Television Standards Committee. Sometimes humorously referred to as Never the Same Color.

One shot An audio file that does not contain looping information but is intended to play once, not necessarily in time.

Output Getting audio out of the computer to an analog speaker, digital output via SPDIF, AES/EBU, or other file format external to the computer.

P-frame In interframe compression schemes such as MPEG, the predictive video frame that exhibits the change that occurred compared to the I-frame before it. See I-frame and B-frame.

Pad Attenuation of the original audio level. See Attenuation.

PAL Phase Alternation Line. Most all countries use PAL outside of the U.S. and Japan. Sometimes jokingly referred to as Picture at Last.

Pan Panorama, or moving audio across the audio spectrum left to right, front to back, or a combination of both. Each channel in most NLEs and DAWs offer a pan control that may be automated.

Peak Audio level's maximum point in a file.

Pillarbox The opposite of letterbox, where black masks are inserted on the sides of an image.

Playback Listening or monitoring the recording after it's been written to hard drive or tape; reviewing the audio file as it's being composed, also referred to as "previewing." That makes no sense, because you are not viewing the video or audio prior to any edit, you are listening or watching video post-edit, making the term "preview" inaccurate.

Playhead Where the cursor lies within the DAW or NLE application as relevant to a timeline. "Cursor" and "playhead" are generally interchangeable. In most applications, the playhead is indicated by the vertical line moving across the screen.

Playlist A set of instructions that tell a linked video how to behave, which audio it should use, when it should play, and what follows after its playback.

Plug-in A DAW or NLE term referring to audio or video processors that may be used to supplement the application's audio or video editing tools.

Preset Predetermined parameters of a plug-in, template, or other predetermined setting for an application.

Preview Viewing or listening to media from an application. Preview is defined by watching video associated with a project and listening to audio loops or compositions assigned to the video, or listening to playback of a musical composition with or without video. See Playback.

Project A collection of audio and video files to be assembled for a final product.

RAM Random Access Memory.

Region A predetermined space and time on the Timeline in any DAW or NLE application, controlling playback area and time. It can also mean a segment of audio or video that may be separately managed for editing.

Render To blend all multimedia files together in one master file format. It is akin to baking a cake from all its individual ingredients.

RGB Red, Green, Blue.

Roll-off The point at which frequencies are filtered out. A low frequency roll-off will rapidly diminish frequencies beginning at the specified point. See Attenuation.

Rumble Low frequencies that are too low to actually be clearly heard but that take up audio information space. Footsteps, vibrations, and motors all create rumble. Many mixing and recording consoles incorporate rumble filters, set to approximately 60–75Hz, rolling low frequencies off at that point to clean up audio. See Roll-off.

SACD Super Audio Compact Disk, a format developed by Sony and Philips. These disks offer a superior format of recording including multichannel.

Sample rate The interval and resolution at which audio is "photographed" or measured. Audio CDs are sampled at a rate of 44.1kHz and 16 bits. Most NLEs and DAWs are capable of much higher resolutions and sample rates.

Session A space of time dedicated to recording audio. Each time a new recorded file is created, it may be referred to as a session. Digidesign's ProTools uses this term for their basic document of assembled elements.

SFX Sound effects.

Sibilance The hissing sounds of the human voice, most noticed in Ss, Ps, and Ts. High frequencies are sometimes challenging to control. Use a DeEsser plugin or an EQ to control this phenomenon.

Slug A blank area left on a Timeline for later insertion of media.

SMPTE Society of Motion Picture and Television Engineers. Also used as a timecode reference.

Solo A button or switch that allows a single channel to be monitored. Mutes all other audio during playback when engaged.

Source audio Audio from the original program media. In a video file, this is on-location sound, or audio related to the original source and is often replaced or enhanced.

Spot Announcement for broadcast, e.g., a commercial.

Spotting Identifying and documenting cues for music, effects, sound design, or other audio information. See Cue.

Stem Audio components such as dialog, music, and effects.

Stereo Two-channel audio, consisting of similar or dissimilar audio spread across the left-to-right spectrum. Two separate mono channels separated to one left and one right would not be considered stereo but rather dual mono. Stereo mixes consist of placing elements on the multitrack timeline in representations of their occurrence across the left-to-right spectrum, and then mixed to a two-channel mix reflecting the positioning of audio elements.

Streamer A slug or graphic overlay on video playback, marking exact points that a cue is to take place. Functions as a visual hit point or cue. See Cue.

Subwoofer Speaker enclosure optimized to reproduce sounds from 20Hz to 125Hz.

Surround sound Multichannel audio that emanates from multiple sources, usually set equidistant from the listener's position. Often related to 5.1 sound, surround can be quadrophonic, or as large as any number of speaker sources might be employed, so long as they are all emitting unique audio from each source.

S-video Short for super video, a technology used for transmitting video signals over a cable by dividing the video information into separate signals: one for luma and one for chroma. (S-video is synonymous with Y/C video). S-video is a consumer form of component video used primarily with Hi8 and S-VHS equipment.

Sweet spot The prime listening area between two speakers in a stereo environment or a 5.1 listening environment. The sweet spot is the point where all audio channels are most precise, arriving at the same location at the same time. It is a relatively small area in most any listening environment.

Sweeten Polishing or improving an existing recording through adding other parts to the composition or audio elements. Processing of sound is also considered sweetening. Anything done to original audio in order to enhance it's quality.

Sync Synchronize, to ensure that events occur at the same time. Timecode is generally a common source to ensure events are in sync.

T/C Timecode.

Temporal compression A compression method that reduces the data contained within a single video frame by identifying similar areas between individual frames and eliminating the redundancy. See also Codec and MPEG.

Timeline A component of a DAW or NLE where graphic and video elements are placed for purposes of inclusion on the DVD or CD. Timelines include audio, video, and graphic elements.

Track An individual line containing audio loop elements.

Transfer rate How fast a disk drive or CD drive can transfer information to the CPU. May be a burst rate or sustained rate. High cache levels (8MB) or larger assist in providing information to the CPU at fast rates, important when building large compositions or FX sequences in the NLE, lots of audio tracks in the DAW, and deep menu structures in DVD authoring.

Transient The difference between the lowest point of decay and highest point of attack in an audio file.

Transport Play, record, stop, rewind, fast forward, record are all functions of the Transport in an NLE or DAW. The Transport tools control position of playback and the playhead.

Treble The high end of the audio frequency spectrum, generally 2kHz and above.

Two-pass An encoding feature allowing video to be scanned prior to encoding. During the first pass, the encoder determines how it will allocate bits during the encoding process. It results in slower encodes but generally higher quality in high-motion video.

Underscore Background music, not necessarily musically composed, to create an emotional atmosphere or environment. Underscore is similar to, and often called, a music bed. See Bed.

Upconvert A term used to describe the conversion of a lower resolution to a higher number, such as "upconverting" 720p to 1080i. This is a misnomer though, since to accomplish a quality upsample the horizontal scanning frequency is actually lowered from 45kHz to 33.75kHz. The quality of resolution is not improved by this method, and it's more appropriate to describe upconverting as "re-conforming."

USB Universal Serial Bus.

Video file In the video world this is relevant to QuickTime, .mpg, .wmv, avi, m2t, or m2v files, data files that contain video information.

Volume The indicator for the overall level of a loop, track, or master project output level.

Wave (.wav)-The Microsoft designator for audio file formats, a common file type. Used by Windows applications as a file format.

Workspace The primary work surface in an NLE or DAWs main window, where most of the work is performed.

You've Seen the Future.
Now Meet the Artists Who Are Making It.

VASST is Video, Audio, Surround, and Streaming Training. Here at VASST we help you master your preferred topic faster than you ever expected with immediate, accessible and thorough information. We offer a variety of training materials for different learning styles.

Whether you are looking for a book, a DVD, or an on-site trainer, VASST can provide tips, techniques, and solutions for all your media needs.

VASST Training Tours: visit vasst.com for current tour dates. We offer seminars on Cameras, Lighting, Editing, Surround Sound, and other general media topics. Training on specific applications by companies such as Adobe, Sony, Ulead, Pinnacle, AVID, Boris, and Apple is also available.